Beyond the Gray Leaf

The Life and Poems of J.P. Irvine

Dustin Renwick

Beyond the Gray Leaf: The Life and Poems of J.P. Irvine is a work of nonfiction.

Copyright © 2016 Dustin Renwick

Published by Fleetwing Books
www.fleetwingbooks.com

ISBN-10: 0-9976265-9-3
ISBN-13: 978-0-9976265-9-9

Cover design by Whitney Fenzel

DEDICATION

For Lou Ann, because she asked
(among other good reasons)

CONTENTS

Fate is common, though unseen,
Walk we all the self-same way;
In the spring the leaves are green,
In the fall they're just as gray.

– excerpt from "Prelude"
in *The Green Leaf and the Gray*

INTRODUCTION

This book started when my uncle bought a school.

No children had entered the building in decades, and the village had abandoned the property. We walked the halls when my family visited during the holidays. I found a book in the cool silence of a dusty classroom.

The *Green Leaf and the Gray,* bound in mottled maroon, bore the name of an author from Kirkwood, Illinois, a tiny town a few miles from my childhood home in Monmouth.

Someone had tucked into the book a browned newspaper clipping that detailed the death of a well-known poet.

I had never heard of J.P. Irvine, but fame doesn't always prevent forgetting.

Western Illinois has its quota of prominent poets just with Carl Sandburg's birthplace. Still, Irvine had apparently merited some bygone notoriety.

Several years passed, at which point I had undertaken a comprehensive genealogy of my family. I rolled around for a month deep in the historical muck of census reports, courthouse documents, and internet searches. I tossed Irvine's name into the mix somewhere in the process, and I didn't stop pulling the threads until I had quilted a timeline of his life and the major characters in it.

He grew up on the Illinois prairies, but he didn't stay put. He appears to have lived for short stints in Springfield and Chicago, the state's capital and capital of commerce, respectively. He also traveled the country, from Niagara Falls to Colorado.

But it was the few years in Washington, DC, that altered his life.

He read a poem titled "Unknown" in front of President Ulysses S. Grant and 10,000 participants at Decoration Day 1873. The spark of notoriety and Irvine's potential relationships with literary figures in the city improved his reception. Capital newspapers subsequently published his pieces, as did some of the major literary magazines of the time.

Yet Irvine published only one book, and it didn't include the text for "Unknown," arguably his most significant work. *The Green Leaf and the Gray* appeared in May 1891, a year before his death. A few anthologies collected Irvine's poems for about a decade, and then obscurity arrived in such thorough fashion that none of my teachers ever mentioned the local poet's existence.

So 125 years later, where does Irvine's legacy stand?

I contend that his oblivion is not a function of his importance. After all, he presented original poetry to a U.S. president. That moment alone held enough significance to justify my foray into the past to find those lost words.

One good day with the president doesn't make him a nationally significant author, but we should extend a halo of historical relevance for his role as a prominent regional writer in an era when Midwestern authors strived to differentiate their collective voice from the bastions of literary aristocracy in the East.

He excelled in his portrayals of the Civil War, and the *Chicago Tribune* called some of his nature poems "nearly pure gold." But the selections he chose to include in his book hardly represented his best work, to the detriment of his reviews then and the memory of his contributions now.

The Green Leaf and the Gray contained 40 poems and one untitled fragment. I reclaimed more than double that number of poems and letters locked among thousands of microfilmed newspaper pages.

This book offers a curated selection of Irvine's poetry paired with the historical and biographical context of his life. School not included.

– Dustin Renwick, 2016

NOTES ABOUT THE TEXT

No. 1
Irvine published multiple versions of some poems with minor changes in word choices. I've presented a few of these as a blend of their forms.

No. 2
You'll notice [illegible] sometimes. That indicates words I couldn't decipher, often caused by the fold lines in 150-year-old newspapers, which transform into devilish cross-hatched blurs when converted to microfilm.

No. 3
English, like any good language, is not as fixed as dictionaries would have us believe. A living, morphing lexicon means Irvine used words that have fallen from favor in modern times or mean something quite different. I've highlighted these cases in *italics* before the poems.

FAMILY CHATS

Whether you plan for months or outright ignore it, your birthday has a strong connection to you aside from marking the moment you entered the world. Governments and businesses require you to share that string of numbers to keep moving through daily life. James P. Irvine would have a problem.

Various obituaries list his date of birth on May 12 or May 18. His death certificate splits the difference at May 16. The sources at least agree on the year 1836. But his tombstone shows a clearly carved 1835.

His parents were David (1801-1890) and Jane (Davidson) Irvine (1805-1893). David was the first generation of the Irvine line born in America as both parents were native Irish. Jane's father was born Pennsylvania, and her mother was born in Ireland. The Irvine parents both reached age 88 with the blessing of long lives and the curse of burying nearly all their children.

James — his middle name remains a mystery — was the eldest child, born in central Pennsylvania near Shaver Creek, in Huntingdon County. A trio of brothers arrived in quick succession. Robert (1836-1896), John (1838-1877), and David (1839-1864).

The family moved to Illinois in 1842 or 1843, depending on the source, as some of the earliest settlers of Warren County and what would become the town of Kirkwood. The children numbered seven after Edwin (1842-1882), Bell (1844-1871), and Sara Jane (1847-1927).

Whew. Let's take a break after that blur of numbers. This book focuses on James by both choice and necessity. He left breadcrumbs. Most of the siblings now persist in the shadows as far as records are concerned. This makes their lives not less noteworthy but less traceable.

Robert proves the slight exception because he appears in plenty of local newspaper briefs. They depict him as a playful rabble-rouser and an expert tiddlywinks player. He produced memorable commentary like his report that "fish are so thick in the stream at Coghill's mill . . . the boat has to be slid over the backs of the fish."

This opening poem provides a catalog of the Irvine family, a wonderful resource for biographical details but not for first-class poetry. Many pieces in this section reflect almost hagiographic terms for relatives and friends. His sentimental style, offered in an elementary ABCB rhyme for each four-line chunk, contributed to much of the criticism James received in reviews of his book. The book was published at the end of the 19th century, when poetic values in America had shifted away from the idealistic treatments and formal structures of romanticism.

That's also the last time you'll see James — self-referenced as Jim in the following poem. He opted for his initials by at least 1855, the date of his first published poem I could find.

Burthen is an archaic form of burden.

A Golden Wedding

Tonight we turn and feign would call
To mind the smiles and tears
That flecked with dappled light and shade
A life of fifty years —
A wedded life of willing hands
That drudged from sun to sun,
And each succeeding morn anew
Took up the work undone.

'Twas plow and plant and gather in,
Again to plow and sow;
The threaded shuttle through the loom

Went ever to and fro;
It was a constant treadmill tramp —
Around and still around;
And though the mill forever went,
The grist was never ground.

But this were well, for, as the times
And seasons kept their speed,
Came restless little feet to shoe,
And little mouths to feed —
Mouths craving bread, and busy hands
In every mischief thrust;
They made the usual pies of mud
And pattered in the dust.

To fall and stub the bootless toes
Was ever boyhood's fate,
And fingers just as sure were pinched
While swinging on the gate;
The smoothly polished cellar-door
Was proof beyond a doubt
Of how the pants were worn in holes
Below the roundabout.

Yet there was mother, deft and quick
To knit and darn and mend;
She soothed the ache and bound the bruise
Her love was without end.

With constant care her faithful eye
Was never turned away
From watching o'er the truant feet
So prone to run astray.

The first one born was little Jim
A most precious chick;
The classic precinct of his birth
Was down on "Shaver's Crick."
At times across his back and legs —
To cure the itch of sin —
Was lain the rod's corrective salt
They must have rubbed it in!

But as he grew he often caught
A glimpse of sunny gleams,
And heard the pulsing silver sounds
Within the land of dreams;
And in the night, when all was still,
Lay musing late and long,
Until he caught the magic spell
And wove them into song.

The next on deck was wayward Bob,
The drollest of the crew.
How often! oh, how often
Has he pinched us black and blue!
He went in manhood to the war,

And fought as he had pinched,
And when a bullet pierced his thigh
He swore but never flinched.

And then poor John in order came,
Kindhearted, dashing, free;
I never knew of one so full
Of sanguine hope as he —
A hope that turned aside and smiled
At grim misfortune's frown,
Until, alas! in dark eclipse
His noon-day sun went down.

And there was David, who, when grown,
In manly beauty stood
A type of rounded strength, as stands
A young oak in the wood.
His heart was glad, and when the drums
Were beating far and wide,
He marched — a soldier — to the front
And, fighting, fell and died.

The next was Edwin, who from birth
Walked in his Maker's ways,
And kept in simple, faithful trust
His precepts all his days;
And when at length a dread disease
Its fatal course began,

He met it — dying as he lived —
At peace with God and man.

Then Bell in turn — a laughing lass —
One summer's day was born
The light that lit her nature seemed
A reflex of the morn.
Consumption! dread destroyer!
Thou hast claimed her for thine own.
White souls there are; a whiter one
Than hers I've never known.

Then on one snowy New Year's eve
In came a gift from heaven;
'Twas little, brown-eyed Sara Jane,
The best of all the seven.
A faithful daughter she has been,
A sister true and sweet;
Her feet were swift to run, her heart
In loyal kindness beat.

In mother's stead she sewed and baked,
And scoured and cleansed the cup;
In sickness bathed the fevered brow
The faint head lifted up.
And still she's here to-night to share
The burthens yet unborne —
The strength and stay of these old forms

So weary and outworn.

So weary with the dizzy whirl
The turmoil and the strife,
The aches, the longings and the cares
Of this uneasy life;
So weary trudging up the hill,
So weary plodding down,
So broken underneath the cross.
So anxious for the crown.

Ah, well! we know the crown's in store;
The rugged path you trod.
And, oh! it must be beautiful —
The city of our God.
Has life not sweets to lure you still?
The loved ones power to bless?
Long as we may for heavenly halls,
We love not earth the less.

Oh, then, dear heaven! hold not thy charms,
And let the sun benign
In Indian summer loveliness
Upon them softly shine;
Stay winter's coming, and when come
Keep back the fall of snow.
We'll love and bless them while they stay,
And bless them when they go.

Irvine didn't fit the idealized modern molds of either a writer who lives as a recluse or a writer who revels in sexual freedom and independence. He instead occupied the end of the spectrum appropriate for the era, as a family man. He also ended up as the sole sibling to raise children. The rest of his brothers and sisters died unmarried or died before they had kids.

The short poem here describes Irvine's wife. Harriett Newell Magennis was born in New York in 1834. She and her sister boarded there in Chautauqua County as late as 1855. When her sister married and lived in Warren County, Harriett moved as well. The nuptial announcement in 1861 described the talents of her and her husband. "For 'Rhyming' and 'Painting' have met in the wedding. And the 'happy result' we trust will be known."

Unfortunately not.

FOR THE BACK OF A PHOTOGRAPH

The brush may err but not the art
That paints with sunbeams; here you trace
The very thoughts upon your face,
So clearly cut in every part
And well defined in every grace
The subtlest feature, unconcealed,
Your living presence stands revealed.

An 1861 advertisement in *The Monmouth Atlas* listed Irvine's services as an attorney in town. He and Harriett relocated in 1864 to Rockford, Illinois, near the Wisconsin border. They lived at 117 North Third Street, a few blocks east of the Rock River that divides the city north to south.

Irvine had become a recognizable local writer for his poems printed in Warren County newspapers, but he added the operations and business side of newspaper publishing. Founder and editor Irvine released the first issue of *The Winnebago Chief* on November 21, 1866, with the motto: "Hew to the line, let the chips fall where they will!" Praise and congratulations arrived from fellow broadsheets across the state.

"We certainly wish it unbounded success, not only from its intrinsic merit, but also from feelings of strong personal friendship for the editor," wrote *The Monmouth Atlas*, a publication with like-minded Republican leanings.

"We wish him, sincerely, the most complete success in all things save his political opinions," ribbed *The Monmouth Review*. "He is not too old to learn, however, and we will not yet despair of some day beholding him advocating political truth."

Irvine added Hiram Enoch, an area printer, to the masthead the following July, and they changed the paper's name to *Winnebago County Chief* with the August 1 issue. Enoch lasted a little more than a year, and then Irvine continued solo, though likely shrewder after tapping Enoch's expertise.

All told, the move had resulted in a few years of happy prosperity for the Irvines, a family of three with their first child, Elizabeth. Then Little Lizzie died in summer 1869 after being thrown from a runaway carriage. Irvine reflects on his daughter in this poem. The repetition of snow at the end of each stanza would have achieved an even more profound effect if he had carried that arrangement through to the concluding line.

Irvine sold his newspaper to Enoch a year later and wrote about his fortunes in his farewell letter. "I had not the money to sustain it, and a lack of money and hard times and domestic trials and afflictions, crushed my ambitions until I became aware that I was neither doing my patrons justice nor carrying out the intent of my motto."

Enoch released the first issue of the new *Rockford Journal* on October 29, 1870. A successor later sold the paper to the *Rockford Morning Star*, which eventually led to the city's modern paper, the *Rockford Register-Star*.

Despite the sorrowful circumstances, economic troubles weren't particular to Irvine's publication. He mentioned the "notorious fact that people do not pay the printer with that promptness they do others." Newspapers arrived and folded with regularity in that era, but overall, the industry grew. By 1880, Illinois had more than 1,000 newspapers and at least one in every county — double the number in 1870, when Irvine left the *Chief* and headed east.

My Little Girl Under the Snow

I am standing alone by the window
A looking out on the infinite gray,
As it deepens and darkens to silence
At the close of a desolate day:
There's a lull in the sleeting and raining,
And now in the stillness I know —
As the flakes feather aimlessly downward —
That all the night long it will snow.

And lo, as it falls in the valley,
In the deep, still woods and the sea,
There's a fall, as of flakes, in the darkness
Of the life that God gave unto me;
For the clouds have been heavy and rainy,
But now there's a lull, and I know
That my sorrow is soft'ning to longing
For my little girl under the snow.

This night, for my poor little darling,
In her little grave under the leaves,
Only dressed in a shroud of Swiss-muslin,
Cut low at the neck and the sleeves;
For she died when the manifold lilies
Were a-bloom in the garden below,
But the meek little face in the coffin
Was as mute and as pure as the snow.

And now, I remember, while thinking,
How a year ago — this very night,
That she and I, here by the window,
Stood watching the snow-birds alight;
And coaxingly calling she fed them
With little white pellets of dough,
But alas, did I think that my birdie
Would sleep to-night under the snow.

But why should I weary with longing,
When to cease, if for e'en but a day
Or a night, would be proof of forgetting;
Ah, sorrow, stay with me, I pray;
Stay with me, that I may be humble
And patient in bearing the loss
Of the dear little idol that keeps me,
So near to the foot of the cross.

Irvine spent three years in Washington, DC, after Rockford. That time changed his life in many ways, but it's a period we'll visit later. When he returned to western Illinois, Irvine found a successful general store in Kirkwood operated by a family that boasted some catchy names and a wide geographic range.

Moses Allen was born in Massachusetts and his wife, Minerva Fletcher, hailed from Vermont. They reached Warren County in 1864 from the Rockford area, just as Irvine made the reverse commute. When Moses died in 1881, Irvine wrote a lengthy obituary about the man — by that point, the patriarch of trusted family friends.

The eldest Allen child, Henry, traveled between Illinois and the Colorado mines in the early 1880s. He served two terms as a representative in the Illinois General Assembly later in the decade before another push west. In 1890, Henry worked as a book keeper and tonnage clerk for the Southern Pacific Railroad in San Francisco.

His younger sister Ina beat him to the ocean. She married in Illinois, and they moved to San Francisco, where her husband worked as a cable car conductor. Another younger sister, Oskie, lived in Boston for a year to study music, but she and her mother soon headed for California too. Much of the family remained on the coast for the rest of their lives, including Minerva, who had covered the entire continent in her lifetime.

Irvine formed a close relationship with Henry, and the two traveled together and hosted local dinner parties when they both lived around Kirkwood. Henry had accumulated a fortune in Berkeley real estate by the time he died in 1922. The dedication page in *The Green Leaf and the Gray* read: "To Henry W. Allen of San Francisco, Cal., The best of friends and companions I dedicate this volume."

This poem, written for Ina, uses a simple ABAB rhyme, but exceeds Irvine's typical barrier of personal affection by reaching for the more inclusive commentary on the passage of time.

Hie is a verb meaning to move quickly.

FROM THE ALBUM OF MISS INA ALLEN

My friend! your life is in the May,
The wine of spring is in your veins;
And like this virgin page, I pray,
It e'er may be as free from stains.

Ah, me! but May is fleet of wing;
She is too sweet to go so soon, —
We hardly hear the robins sing
Before she hies away to June.

Though June is dear, we sigh withal
Amid her lavish sweets to know
That summer nimbly seeks the fall;
Then comes the winter with its snow.

Still, when the winter of your years
Shall come, 'twill sweeter be than spring;
'Tis peaceful age alone that hears
From earth the bells of heaven ring.

Developing new friendships throughout life keeps a person vibrant, but the oldest friends rely on time-tested bonds. Irvine welcomed the Allens; he grew up with Joseph Leeper.

The families lived next door to each other in Kirkwood. All five Irvine brothers and Leeper registered for the Civil War draft together in summer 1863. John, Edwin, and J.P. signed up for the first time. Robert, David, and Jo Leeper re-enlisted as veterans. Leeper served with the 83rd Illinois Infantry, a regiment that cemented its reputation earlier that year at the battle of Fort Donelson in Tennessee. Irvine would later memorialize that battle in one of his poems, doubtless after hearing stories from his friend.

Leeper survived the Confederate guns only to die by a different bullet. He returned to Kirkwood after the war and drove farm animals as a teamster. He moved to Dakota — just Dakota back then — in 1881. When a nephew visited, the two headed for a hunting trip. The nephew's gun discharged, and hit Leeper in the left shoulder. The doctor didn't judge the wound to be serious, but Leeper died 11 days later, on Halloween 1888.

Irvine employs mostly rhyming couplets in the elegy to his friend, but the poem would have offered a stronger emotional punch had it ended midway with the sentence about him and Jo.

Instead, Irvine spends another 14 lines pontificating on Leeper's virtues. The general observations dampen the impact of the first half and drag a good poem into ho-hum territory.

He ends the piece with a faith-based reference, a common theme in Irvine's work. David and Jane joined as charter members of United Presbyterian Church in Kirkwood, and the entire family attended.

A rick is a stack of crops.

Jo Leeper

Forty years ago, or nigh,
Barefoot boys were Jo and I.
I a child and he a child,
Here, when all the grove was wild;
Played together every day —
In the straw rick, in the hay;
Hunted birds' eggs, went to school,
And a-swimming in the cool,
Deep, delicious willow pool
Now dried up, with just the stumps
To show where grew the willow clumps.
There's change! The creek sinks in its bed;
I am tired and Jo is dead.
He so lithe and fleet and strong,
Built, we thought, for living long.

Better boy was never known,
Nor a better man when grown;
Kindly-hearted, boy-like still,
Thought no evil, spake no ill,
Peaceable — he knew no strife,
Even-tempered all his life.
Loved to romp and laugh and joke,
Uncomplaining took the yoke
When others fainted. Noble heart!
Well he filled a brother's part.
Lay him gently down to rest;
He deserves it; God knows best.

Excitement and doldrums, joy and sadness — much of life happens in the mundane details between these extremes. After he moved back to Kirkwood from the nation's capital, Irvine lived a recognizable life. He repainted his cottage when it needed the work. He visited friends. He complained that "hunters passing to and fro over the sidewalk between town and the cemetery are shooting the walk full of holes."

His house on West Street was situated about a half mile south of Center Grove Cemetery. The Irvine family, beginning with David and Jane, deeded and sold much of the land that established and then expanded the burial ground where they lie today. The proximity of the cemetery mirrors the relationship Irvine's life and poetry shared with the many forms of death.

This poem explores that dual narrative. Some might criticize the uncomplicated ABAB rhymes, but Irvine balances the form with the subject matter: the inevitable fate that awaits everyone and a question of how we spend our lives in the meantime. The town below, and the town above.

Kirkwood formed from the prairies of Irvine's childhood into a community tied to the commerce of the Mississippi River by way of the railroad. The Chicago, Burlington, and Quincy line, known as the CB&Q, cut a northeast-southwest diagonal through Kirkwood. The town sat 200 miles from Chicago but just 20 miles from the river and the port at Burlington, Iowa.

Increased prosperity in the town brought infrastructure improvements, not all of which Irvine welcomed. Road commissioners moved Irvine's fence further in on his property to expand West Street. The former attorney countered with legal action, which delighted the small-town gossip grapevine.

The street "still obstinately refuses to retire to the background, as any respectable, well-ordered street would do. . . . The suit comes off, Saturday, and promises to be a lively one." Within a week, however, the department had paid Irvine's claims and snuffed the predicted festivities. What didn't change was the location of his house, and Irvine could at any time look north and see his second home.

TWO TOWNS

My cottage crowns a knoll of land,
And peering upward through the green
Of maple boughs — on either hand
Its dormer-windows may be seen.

And there it is when looking down,
The season long in sun or rain,
You see a thrifty neighbor town
At either ending of the lane.

A narrow lane and travel worn,
From lagging wheels and feet that tread
A-weary with the burdens borne
Between the living and the dead.

Though scarce a furlong either way,
In one I hear the robins sing,
And in the other all the day
The smitten anvil's measured ring —

All day I hear the champ of drills,
The roll of trains and engine-booms;
The low, incessant grind of mills,
The muffled pounding of the looms.

Meet whom ye will, there's none but seems
Pursuing some elusive quest,
Two fretful, counter-passing streams
That never know a moment's rest.

The streets may climb the rugged hill,
Or straggle outward to the plain,

But wind and wind the way they will
They lead at last unto the lane —

The narrow way we all must pass —
How soon or late there's none may know,
Our quiet homes beneath the grass
Are always ready when we go.

No pictures of Irvine have appeared in all my research, but some information exists about his relatives.

Based on Civil War enlistment records, his four brothers were all tall, between 5'8" and 6 feet. All had either gray or blue eyes. No such details exist for Irvine, for reasons covered in the next section of this book. According to his poetry, his sister Sara Jane had brown eyes, but his second daughter, Annabel, had blue eyes like her uncles. Genetic probabilities don't guarantee Irvine's physical traits would have fallen into these patterns, but the available evidence provides possibilities.

His physical condition is more certain.

One poem, "Fever," contains some of the many references to Irvine's nonspecific but lifelong debilitation. For example, *The Monmouth Daily Review* reported that the author would visit the city to sell copies of his book after he recovered from another bout of illness.

The newspaper published the following poem in conjunction with his obituary as an apt description of the author's health troubles. Alas, the piece aspires to nothing more than self-reflection. Irvine's death certificate listed the cause as consumption of several years, but the *Review* added color to the clinical statement.

"[I]t was not till the horizon was streaked with

the roseate hue of the morning that his spirit departed from the tired body. . . . Mr. Irvine had all his life been a great sufferer."

Aye functions as an adverb in this sense, not an exclamation, and means always.

REST

Deep broods the night on land and sea,
As bent and lame I homeward creep,
And fondly lay me down to sleep,
Through all the night-of-years to be.

It is the sleep that lasts for aye,
The balm that heals the hurts of all:
My heavy eye-lids droop and fall,
And all my being swoons away.

O friend, come grant me one request,
Make wide the confines of my tomb,
I am so weary, give me room
To lie full length in blissful rest.

Full length, as on a folded fleece
Around by curtained darkness hung,
Till healed forever and made young
For that new world where all is peace.

WAR ECHOES

So about those blue eyes. Or gray. Or neither. We don't know because Irvine doesn't have a Civil War paper trail like his brothers. Irvine watched all four march off in Union blue: Robert with the 59th Illinois Infantry, John and Edwin with the 138th, and David with the 36th.

Documents show Irvine as the drummer for the Monmouth Reserve Guard drill company in 1861, and remember he registered for the draft in 1863 with his brothers and Jo Leeper. Still, he doesn't appear to have served, likely due to his nagging medical problems.

The National Park Service's database of soldiers and sailors lists one James Irvine from Illinois. He could be the author, but in no other case have I ever found him without a middle initial. He is James P. on the draft list. The man on the NPS roll served with the 134th Infantry organized in Chicago. That regiment mustered for only 100 days of garrison duty in Kentucky.

The war affected Irvine deeply, from his family's grief to the broader distress of the nation, and such sentiment shows in the poems of this section. He writes as though he possessed first-hand experience, but we must conclude that his familiarity with the carnage came via correspondence with his brothers and friends or coverage in newspapers and magazines.

His writings on the topic sometimes repeat the same imagery, but overall the work represents Irvine's best. Haunting lines, visceral descriptions, and immediate observations that develop into common experience all mark the bold, confident writing in his Civil War poetry. This poem provides a good example with a profound reflection on an ordinary musical instrument.

However, various newspapers added to the confusion of his military status when they published his poems. They list him as Comrade Irvine, Maj. Irvine, and even Col. Irvine, a high-ranking title for someone with no apparent war service.

Leal means loyal and honest. Plummet refers to a plumb line.

THE DRUMS

O with pomp of plumes and banners,
Ye may blow your cornets sweet,
But the airs that moved a nation
Were the tunes the drummers beat.

You remember how they thrilled us,
As we heard in other years,
When Rebellion smote the Union,
And she called her volunteers?

How "The Gates of Edinboro,"
For the feet a rhythm played,
And "The Girl I Left Behind Me"
In the heart a swelling made?

How the smith with lifted hammer
Heard a moment, caught the time
Struck his anvil into chorus,
As a ringer rings a chime?

How the mower paused and pondered —
He so young and leal and lithe —
As he tapped a martial ditty,
With his whetstone on the scythe?

And the mason scarce had caught them,
From the keystone on the arch,
Ere he dropped his line and plummet,
And took up his line of march.

Not a loyal ear but hearkened,
Not a soul afraid to dare;
There were pale lads from the counters,
Brave hearts from everywhere.

There were choppers from the timber,
Leaving half unhewn the sill;
There were plowmen from the furrow,
There were grinders from the mill.

There were fathers, poor and needy,
Brought the help of their old age;
There were sweethearts bade their lovers
Write their names on glory's page.

And among them all a widow
With her eldest and her stay,
How she kissed him as she bless'd him;
And with wet eyes went her way?

Till at length the full battalions
Stood aligned in shining blue,

When the "forward march" was spoken
And the fifes struck up anew

With "The Girl I Left Behind Me" —
And as when the tempest comes —
With rattling hail and thunder-booms
In broke the doubling drums.

Every footfall caught the rhythm,
Every heart in valor beat,
As the column swept unbroken
Like a flood-tide through the street —

Swept unbroken and beyond us,
With the drums still throbbing far,
For the harvest must be gathered
In the scarlet fields of war.

In a war that shattered families both physically and ideologically, the Irvines stood together with the Union. Even if J.P. didn't experience active duty, he broadcast his views in other ways.

He signed a call for a convention in 1861 that aimed to nominate candidates for local and county offices. The account borrowed tones from the Revolutionary War. "Shall there be a triumph by the enemies of liberty, and sadness of heart among the friends of freedom the wide world over . . . ? Well may we be willing to die when all is lost for which it is worthwhile to live." Convention-backed selections swept the November elections. But slavery still blemished the nation. Irvine declared his side again in his writings.

Two newspapers served Monmouth, a few miles from Kirkwood and the seat of Warren County. The *Review* leaned Democratic with mild support for the status quo while the *Atlas* maintained a staunch Republican, anti-slavery view. Both printed Irvine's poems before the country split, but the *Review* shows a conspicuous absence of his work during the conflict.

The rival *Atlas* published Irvine's poems, including this one, throughout the war. Though similar to the poem about his young daughter's death, here Irvine fulfills the effect of repetition in the final lines of each stanza. This piece highlights a move toward free verse, some of his early experimentation with new poetic forms — namely, anything beyond the predictable rhymes that produced the most persistent criticisms of his work.

A lea is an area of open grass or cropland.

THE SLAVE'S LAMENTATION

I
An aged slave lamenting,
And crowned with locks of snow,
Came wandering from a planter's field
With palsied steps and slow;
And the sun was setting golden —
Setting golden in the west —
And the parent bird returning
To her offspring in the nest;
But the poor old man, so weary,
Sat down beneath a tree,
There standing lone and royal,
And wept for liberty.

II
Full well he spake the language
Of a tutored English tongue,
For long his Afric speech had ceased
Its native course to run;

But an Afric heart was beating —
Beating swiftly, beating time —
With a soul that stung with anguish,
As the conscience for a crime;
For the fetters — for the fetters —
Of a master's stern decree,
With the iron links of bondage
Had chained his liberty.

III
The soul, the throne of conscience
And the brain and heart akin,
Were the promptings of a monster
That dwelt his frame within;
It told his ear to listen
To the freeman's joyous song,
And his eye to watch the banner
With the stars and stripes thereon;
To mark the independent,
The glorious and the free,
The heart and hand of union,
The strength of liberty.

IV
How the eagle free on mountain
Unfurls his daring wing,
And soars to meet the thunder cloud
To bathe his plumage in;

How he darts along the valley
And around the woodland side,
And through the hazy distance
In all his kingly pride;
Through the hazy distance
And o'er the rolling sea,
Then upward wheeling greets the sun
In glorious liberty.

V
On the hillside sport the lambkins,
And in the meadows play;
They're free — they bear no tyrant's chains,
They feel no master's sway;
Athletic bounds the timid roe
The verdant landscape o'er,
And through the forest broad and deep
That skirts the ocean's shore;
And there beyond the billows leap
And whirl to meet the lea,
And wildly lash the pebbled strand
In sportive liberty.

VI
And while he thus was musing,
The wings of night unfurled,
And golden sank the setting sun
And pulseless lay the world;

But he was still and pulseless
And death's cold mantle wore,
For best it doth befit the one
[illegible]
No golden hue is worn by death
So dark and stern is he,
'Tis only for the king of day
And gems of liberty.

VII
And thus his chains and fetters,
Which he from childhood wore,
Had purchased him a mantle
From the "night's Plutonian shore,"
Which he wears beside the waters
That lash the sable strand;
Now holding strange communion
With the pale and ghostly band;
And near the planter's field
Still remains the royal tree,
Where the aged slave lamenting,
Wept for liberty.

As the war dragged on, it would deliver glory and grief to the Irvine family within two weeks.

David S. Irvine attended Washington College in Washington, Iowa, in 1855-56. That stands as the single record of the family in higher education, though J.P. lived with him at the time and might have enrolled in the now-defunct school. David continued his studies at Monmouth College in 1859-60. Then he enlisted, one of 232 who left the school for the battlefields.

Fourteen students, including David, served in Company C, the local unit of the 36th Illinois Infantry. Only one, Lieut. William Mitchell, survived the war without physical injuries. "Franklin was the hardest battle I ever saw," he wrote. Lieut. James Wilson, the company commander, matched that judgment: "I have never seen men fight with such determined bravery in my life."

Irvine's ode memorializes the battle and bravery in a ballad.

Within an hour of the opening rifle volleys, Gen. John Bell Hood's Confederate army overwhelmed the Union units stationed forward of the main federal positions and attacked the primary defensive entrenchments. Union Col. Emerson Opdycke led the First Brigade of the Second Division. That group included the 36th, the famed

Fox River Regiment. Opdycke had held his men in reserve behind the front, and when the soldiers in gray broke the blue lines, the First Brigade rushed to fill the gap.

At least two generals credited the First Brigade, and particularly the 36th, with turning the battle in favor of the North. A regimental history published in 1876 quoted an Army of the Cumberland historian: "[S]eldom in the history of war has a single brigade made itself so conspicuous in saving an army." That text also contained the quote from Opdycke that Irvine used in this poem.

FRANKLIN, TENN.
NOVEMBER 30, 1864

Hard pressed, we fell back upon Franklin, called a halt
And broke ground in hot haste, to withstand the assault
That we knew would be swift as a whirlwind, and fought
Without quarter.

Howe'er, we were vet'rans, and wrought
As for life; fences were leveled, bridges seized, aids
Sent with sharp orders, trains hurried forward, brigades

Double-quick'd to the trenches where batteries
were set
With the guns loaded plumb to the muzzles, and
yet,
Not a moment too soon!

For the foe had been massed
And were dark'ning the hills, and although we had
passed
Through a hundred encounters, a hush as
profound
As the silence of death brooded ominously 'round,
As we stood in amaze and beheld the dark sweep
Of battalions, interleagued to battalions — six deep
Aye, the whole rebel army, pouring forth from the
wood,
Forty thousand, in battle array under Hood,
Forty thousand, a gray and grim steel-fronted host
Sweeping forward, as dark waters sweep to the
coast
Ere dashed into breakers, until they, with a shout,
Like the noise of the sea in its fury, broke out
And leaped forward!
And yet, there we stood helpless, nor dared fire a
shot:
Two brigades by a blunder misplaced had been
caught
Right between the two fronts, nor were cleared

from the way
Till hundreds fell captive, and the onsetting fray
Struck the works by the pike and poured through,
when Opdycke
Caught a glance of the route, and flashing his blade
From the scabbard, called out to as game a brigade
As ever faced bullets, "Up and at them, my men!"
When the lightnings leaped forth, and it
thundered, and then
To the bayonets bent, right forward we broke
Through the hail-whistling flame of their volleys
and smoke,
Till we met with a clash in a hand-to-hand fight,
Beat them back foot by foot, through the breach,
yet in spite
Of the might of our valor, and the roar and the rack
Of that tempest of death, they wheeled round in
their track —
All afire from our cannon — and again and again
Re-enforced with dark masses of oncoming men
Stormed the line of our works.
Why repeat? You have read of the deeds of that day
In the records of valor; how we held them at bay,
As the sea-walls the breakers; of how they were led
Till the sweeps of their charges were strewn with
the dead;
Of the fronting platoons that were mown from
their feet,

Of the gaps that were filled with no thought of
retreat
Until corps after corps were bereft of the pride
Of their heroes: of how they were shot from astride
The embankments, cut down in the breach, in their
raids
On the colors, 'round the guns, till their scattered
brigades
Could be rallied no longer, and stricken and sore,
With their captains unhorsed and their swiftest no
more,
Their banners in tatters, their standards in two,
Aye, whipped but not conquered, at last they
withdrew,
And the slain of the Gray and the slain of the Blue,
Were as one as they lay under night's heavy pall
With the flag of the Union afloat over all.

Two Irvines — 1st Sgt. David and 2nd Lieut. Robert — fought at Franklin and then marched toward Nashville to defend the city where their lives would diverge. Lieut. Wilson, commander of Company C in the 36th, wrote to the *Atlas* about his encounter with David.

"He [illegible] before we received the order to charge, David went to the 59th and saw his brother Robert. I noticed two or three times while we were moving forward [illegible] crying and I could see his lips moving. We were at that time on the run, and though I noticed it particularly (for I never observed him affected so before) I could not stop to ask him what it was for and have not learned since. I believe he knew he would be killed."

Robert was shot in the leg on December 16, 1864. David died. From his obituary: "While charging the enemy's works a ball passed through his temples, causing instant death."

The following piece doesn't address his brother directly — a poem with David's name as the title does the trick — and it is stronger because the leading role remains anonymous. This short work, with woe and anxiety laced throughout, finds an incredible analog in the famous column by World War II correspondent Ernie Pyle, called "The Death of Captain Waskow."

THE HALT

The day was lost, and we were sent
In haste to guard the baggage train,
And all the night through gloom and rain
Across a land of ruin went.

But halting once, and only then
We turned aside to let the corps
Of ambulances pass before,
That hauled a thousand wounded men!

And leaning, drowsy and oppressed,
Upon my gun I wondered where
The comrade was I helped to bear,
Slow rearward, wounded in the breast.

When lo! I heard a fainting cry —
As wheels drew near and stopped aside:
"The man in here with me has died,
Oh, lift him out, or I shall die!"

"All right," the one-armed driver said,
"The horse can hardly pull the load,
We leave them all along the road,
It does no good to haul the dead!"

And so we turned by lantern light
And laid him in a gloom of pines,
When came an order down the lines,
"Push on, and halt no more to-night!"

War in 1865 hardly resembled modern conflicts, but one disturbing reality links these experiences across the centuries. A third of the fighters, regardless of skin or uniform color, died or suffered injuries — that's more than a million people. New archival research has identified war wounds that didn't appear on the 19th-century transcripts.

The Civil War created a psychological burden that hid in the diaries of veterans, the minds of insane asylum patients, and the sad choices of suicide victims. The lack of medical understanding and the social stigmas associated with mental health issues contributed to the dismissal of these scars: underestimated, overlooked, or outright ignored. Today, we recognize the symptoms of post-traumatic stress disorder.

From the newspaper accounts of his activities later in life, Robert's leg injury at the Battle of Nashville didn't seriously affect him. That resilience becomes more impressive considering that his regiment led the charge in several major battles and suffered severe losses. Add to that his capture and short imprisonment in Kentucky at the Battle of Perryville.

Irvine steers a solemn subject with a humorous approach and strays from the strict meter of the literary establishment. He breaks the couplet structure with strings of three- and four-line rhymes and even invents a word at one point. As in "Jo Leeper," however, the poem would have succeeded in shorter form. The final four lines glare as unnecessary.

Leal means loyal and honest. Hibernian refers to someone from Ireland. Hove is a disused past tense of heave.

THE WOODEN LEG

Have you heard of the fate of poor Gregory McGreg,
Who was leal to the Union and gave it a leg,
That was shattered away by a piece of a shell,
When the battle was red like a fierce, panting hell?
But a life is a life, so he crept to a wood,
Where he lay in a thicket hard by, in his blood,
Till the enemy yielded and faltered and fled
Where the harvest was gathered of the wounded and dead.
So McGreg was borne off to the hospital then,
On a stretcher between two utility men,
And there doctored and soothed by the kindest of hands,
Through the Christian Commish and the singing of psalms,
Till at last he got well of his anguish and such,

Was discharged and went home 'twixt a staff and a crutch;
But his old Uncle Sam — taking kindly to him —
In his goodness of heart — went and bought him a limb.
'Twas a patent concern — as the stamps on it shows —
Though how to describe it the Lord only knows,
But it bends at the knee and it works at the toes;
It is shapely and smooth — as a woman's but still
It is bloodless and cold, and it has not the will
Of the one which he lost in the fight on the hill;
For the muscles and tendons and nerves and such things
Are inanimate tackle of staples and rings,
And garters elastic and fierce-tempered springs,
And Yankee-clock wheels and bass fiddle strings.
When he walked it came up with a jerk and a twitch,
And then down with a sort of a chuck and a hitch,
But he stumbled along, and was happy and kind,
Till he met with a woman of masculine mind!
She besieged his affections and gave him a banter,
He right-about-faced, and they wedded instanter,
But from loving too quickly they should have refrained,
For the honey-moon filled, but the honey-moon waned.

Soon a captious, cavorting virago she prov'd,
And she made him walk Spanish whenever he moved.
On his works — which she frequently did as Mac said —
With the spittoon, or skillet bombarding his head.
And she ogled him much, and a queer notion took
That McGreg was too thick with the Hibernian cook.
But she flirted herself, hence dare not him chide
For his browsing around just a little outside.
Her fellow was spawn'd in the Arkansas bogs,
Talked "hoss" and delighted in rat-and-tan dogs,
Played poker and sneered at the virtue of women,
In short he was more of a brute than a human.
Well, so things run along — and continued to run,
Till one morning Mac 'rose with the lark and the sun,
When he found — by the gods! that he had but one leg,
And the wooden one missing with Mrs. McGreg.
For shouldered had she both his leg and her cross,
And eloped in the night with the man that talked "hoss,"
So pursuit by McGreg would have all been in vain,
And hence he hopped off on his crutch and his cane,
Hopped off to his breakfast and a hearty meal took,

When he told the whole tale to the Hibernian cook,
When she hove a deep sigh, said "the devil do tell,"
And they winked at each other and said "It is well."

MORAL

[illegible]
When his tormenting spouse and her paramour meet,
And then and there leave him in life's giddy rounds,
With a gushing young cook pouring balm on his wounds.

History is always more complex than a paragraph, but here's a refresher on the war's result. The symbolic end arrived on April 9, 1865, when Gen. Robert E. Lee surrendered his Confederate forces to Gen. Ulysses S. Grant at Appomattox Court House, Virginia. "It would be useless and therefore cruel, to provoke the further effusion of blood," Lee said to his staff.

Still, fighting continued for several months afterward, especially in western parts of the country. The states didn't ratify the 13th Amendment, the official abolition of slavery, until December of that year.

Irvine's experiences with and observations of the Civil War resemble the nation's — the process to remember and forget proceeded slower than anyone planned. Irvine continued to explore the war through poetry for the rest of his life, and it counted as his most frequent topic.

This poem begins with a selection from William Shakespeare's play *Julius Caesar*. After the icon's murder, Mark Antony speaks. His monologue opens with the famous appeal, "Friends, Romans, countrymen, lend me your ears," and concludes with part of the quote Irvine used.

The mix of workaday people and the saintly soldiers makes this piece an interesting microcosm of the poetic schools in 1800s America. Authors in the first half of the century imitated their British forebears in a style called romanticism, which valued the ideal and the heroic, as Irvine presents the soldiers here. Toward the middle and late 19th century, American poetry shifted to emphasize realism, a style that celebrated the ordinary. That thread joins this piece with the characters of the mason and pastor. We'll see more of Irvine's transition later.

Kirkyard is a Scottish term for a church cemetery. Bier is a platform on which a corpse is carried to the grave. Mold — Irvine uses the British spelling — in this sense means loose earth, not fungi. Aye functions as an adverb in this sense, not an exclamation, and means always.

OUR DEAD CAESARS

"BEAR WITH ME, MY HEART IS IN THE COFFIN WITH CAESAR."

I
A stone's throw back from the market road,
An old church stands in the wood hard by,
With a kirk-yard ample and broad,
Where the dead of the neighborhood lie.
And the mason who built those walls —
Grew old, toiling early and late —
Now sleeps where the long shadow falls

From the gable not far from the gate.
And the pious folk say he sleeps well;
That he said, 'ere his spirit had flown,
That the temple wherein he should dwell,
Had Christ for the chief cornerstone.

II
As th' years rolled by with unceasing tread,
The flock and their shepherd met there,
Oft times, alas, to bury the dead,
Or commune with the Father in prayer.
Year after year, on each Holy Day,
The pastor propounded the Word,
Till the gospel seed fell by the way,
And the harvesters gleaned for the Lord.
Reaping thus where the sower had sown,
And gathering the sheaves that were bound,
Till today, under yonder white stone,
The good pastor sleeps in the ground.

III
Blithely and sweetly the wild-thrush sings
In the boughs of the elm tree near;
On the gray church walls the green ivy clings,
As memory encircles the bier.
The wild-thrush sings — Whom cans't it be for?
Ah, my poor heart is heavy today,
I can heed but the thunders of war,

As they heavily roll up the way.
I can see but the yellow clay mounds,
When my soul burrows into the grave,
And there bathes the blood-clotted wounds
Of our dead Caesars sacred and brave.

IV
Their church pews are empty and still,
Their ranks have grown thin — but full grown th'
tomb;
There's a poor widow's cot o'er the hill
Hangs a ball-riddled coat in the room.
In a house at the foot of the lane,
Is a hat that will never be worn,
A Bible deep crimsoned with stain,
And a lock from the smitten head shorn.
There's a sword in yon house to the left,
[illegible] and cracked hilt
But in well-tried steel two rebel skulls cleft,
And the blood of disloyalty spilt.

V
But the true hand that drew it lies cold,
Yet the fire it gleamed forth blazes high,
A million tried boys still troop o'er the mould
With the watch-word — "We conquer or die."
In the old church yard, dear soldiers, sleep well;
May our gratitude grow with the years,

Our hearts like the summer clouds swell,
And we rain out the burden in tears,
May you dwell where the old mason said
He would rest, ere his spirit had flown,
In that temple where Christ at the head
Stands for aye as the chief cornerstone.

Local tributes to the heroes of a recovering nation began almost immediately after the gunfire subsided. The first declared ceremonies for Decoration Day nationwide took place on May 30, 1868. A veterans group called the Grand Army of the Republic established the date. Memorial Day, as it is now called, became a national holiday in 1971.

Irvine often read poems as part of Kirkwood's celebrations of the living and dead patriots. The *Review* reported that his contribution in 1886 was "one of the finest that ever fell from his pen, but the crowd had become restless and tired and did not appreciate it as deserved."

Mediterranean peoples have prized the *Cedrus libani*, or Lebanon cedar, for thousands of years, and part III of the following poem references both the plant and Psalm 104:16. "The trees of the Lord drink their fill, the cedars of Lebanon which he hath planted."

Irvine employs simple rhymes here but links them in varied combinations within each stanza to produce a more complex pattern. Later, the poem switches to a series of quatrains. As with some of his other repeating mechanisms, this ending strives for a goal but falls short because Irvine breaks the construct.

Strew is a verb that means to scatter, most often encountered in its past participle form of strewn.

Asphodels, in literary form, are a flower often connected with death and the afterlife, especially in Greek mythology. Flower-de-luce, more commonly the fleur-de-lis, *is a lily or iris, though likely the latter here with lilies in the preceding line.*

MAY THIRTIETH

I
O comrades though in thick'ning green,
Your lowly graves the grasses screen;
And years are long since last we met,
With all the change that years beget,
There's naught of life or time between
To woo away remembrance yet;
Nor naught that is, nor is to be
Hereafter, shall your valor stain;
For all abundant as the sea,
And steadfast as her broad domain,
So is the Nation's love for thee.

II
And lo! upon this hallowed day —
The sweetest e'er to sorrow born —
We seem to wake afar away,
As oft we woke at early morn
In other years, again to hear
The gath'ring sounds of battle near;

The stormy drum's redoubling beat,
The bugle's swift, defiant peal;
The sharp commands, the hurrying feet
Of must'ring squadrons, as they wheel
And league themselves in grim array,
To storm the valiant hosts of gray!
The word to charge, that breaks the pause
Of dread suspense, the wild huzzahs,
As forth the phalanx springs and runs
Full front upon the flaming guns!
As when against a headland steep
A billow strikes and strews the deep
With warring breakers, even so,
The column breaks against the foe,
When man and man in all the heat
And might of fiery fervor meet,
And hand to hand with naked blade
And bayonet, fight undismayed,
The weaker yielding only when
Have fallen half their valiant men;
Their cannon gone, their colors lost,
They smite for every inch they yield,
Until, alas! at fearful cost
The stronger win the sanguine field.

III
And so a grateful people come,
With martial step to fife and drum,

And cornets sounding silver strains,
Along a thousand crowded lanes;
We come when spring in fullness breathes
The wooing airs of summer's dawn;
With plumes of fir and cedar wreaths
Dark green, that smell like Lebanon;
We come with roses and the bells
Of lilies and with asphodels,
And flower-de-luce in beauty blown,
And violets so frail and dear,
That each beseems a blossomed tear
That God had cherished for His own.

We bring them fresh of tint and hue,
And all aglint with sun-lit dew
And lay them in their sweet perfume
With tender touch on every tomb;
And in lagoons and water-ways,
In lakes and harbors and in bays, —
From every fortress on the steep,
And stately ship where cannon frown
We let a fragrant garland down
For all who slumber in the deep.

Sleep, comrade, sleep, on sea or land,
There's not a palm-full of your clay,
So hidden, but a blossomed spray
Is drop't by some remembering hand.

For thee the healing rains of spring
Fall earlier that the grass may grow;
The flowers in daintier fullness blow,
The robin redbreasts sweeter sing.

For thee we lift the granite high,
The graven urns of marble set;
Their silver lutes the poets fret
To dulcet strains that never die,

Sleep, comrade, sleep, there lurk about
No ambush'd foe to fear or shun,
The Blue and Gray are one-and-one,
And all the fires of camp are out,

Sleep, comrade, sleep, nor dream again
The vague uneasy dreams of life,
Sleep all forgetful of the strife
The sleep that lulls away your pain.

Sleep, comrade, sleep and dream of bliss,
The night of death is calm and deep,
The war is over, sleep the sleep
That wakes no more to weariness.

Sleep, comrade, sleep in earth's green breast,
There's none to trouble, fear no ill,

The night of death is sweet and still,
Sleep on in the eternal rest.

STREET MURMURS

When the Irvines arrived in Illinois in the early 1840s, they found the western prairies plentiful and the habitation sparse. David and Jane had bought 160 acres — that's a quarter-mile square of land — in 1839 when they still lived in Pennsylvania. Their new property became fruitful for more than their immediate family.

A community was platted and filed for record in 1854 on land owned by David and A. G. Kirkpatrick. The Chicago, Burlington, and Quincy Railroad funded several of the first buildings: hotel, restaurant, and of course, railroad depot. The post office was established as Linden but changed to Young America within a few months. That switch lasted less than a generation because of a political reform movement by the same name.

Locals wanted to disassociate themselves from the controversial politics, and they filed a petition to honor Samuel Kirkwood, a former governor of the neighboring state of Iowa. The town adopted its current name with an official notice from the Secretary of State on June 4, 1874. Irvine Street and Kirk Street still exist today.

THE BELLS OF KIRKWOOD

It is eve, and the coming and going
Of cares, since the gray of the morn
Are at rest, and a harmony flowing
From the village comes over the corn;

As a song o'er the sea when the breakers
Are acalm from their turbulent swells,
Soft winged o'er the manifold acres
Flows the sound of the beautiful bells.

And behold, as I list, my behavior
Is softened, as come unto me
Sweet thoughts of an infinite Savior,
On eternity's deep Galilee.

Of the evening my lifetime is bringing,
With a calm that shall woo and enfold
As a garment of peace, of the ringing
Of bells in the city of gold.

John Burroughs, the writer and naturalist, wrote an essay in 1902 about the importance of incorporating ordinary people and events into the poetical canon. More than a call for realism, Burroughs implored writers to look beyond nature to the steam whistles and miners.

"[U]ndoubtedly the difficulty is not in the poverty of the material of to-day, but in the inadequacy of the man . . . [A]ll phases of modern industrial life . . . are available for poetic treatment to him who can bring the proper fund of human association . . ."

Although the CB&Q tracks threaded through Kirkwood during much of Irvine's time in the town, the subject of this piece is the broader expansion of the railroad system. "[T]he poetic note is clearly and surely struck in his stanzas," Burroughs wrote.

President Abraham Lincoln signed the Pacific Railroad Bill in 1862. The legislation awarded two companies incentives for building track: 6,400 acres (later doubled) and $48,000 in government bonds. Per mile. The Central Pacific Railroad Company started from Sacramento and raced east, while Union Pacific broke ground in Omaha and gobbled land west.

Irvine rode the train from Chicago to Omaha and points west on a Rocky Mountain press junket in 1867. At the time, the line ended in Julesburg, Colorado, the site of several skirmishes in previous years between Native American tribes and white settlers building the transcontinental railroad. The town impinged on Irvine's religious sensibilities.

"If I were asked if hell has a geographic location, I think I should render a decision in favor of Julesburg. Sodom was a moral and religious city in comparison . . ."

Yet the terminus represented the epitome of temporary pains. Here today and gone west tomorrow.

"The continuous line of rail grows longer and longer almost as fast as you can walk," Irvine wrote. "The day of our arrival 4 1/2 miles of track was laid and completed."

Central Pacific met Union Pacific in 1869 to drive a golden spike in the connection point at Promontory Summit, Utah. The engineering and construction feat transformed months-long treks into a few days of travel and reduced the cost of that travel by an exponent. But it also included high-level corruption, broken treaties and massacres of Native Americans, and vicious racism and maltreatment of Chinese workers. Irvine avoids the nuances and negatives in favor of a more romantic treatment that succeeds because of its vivid language and imagery.

Riven *is a synonym for split. Mazy means labyrinthine, but Irvine seems to use the word to describe the corn and farmland as an alteration of maize, suggested by the fields in the preceding line.*

THE LIGHTNING EXPRESS

I
Swift as the wind's untrammeled speed,
A train of chariots, all a length
Of splendor rolls behind a steed
With loins of iron and the strength
A legion horses; and as breaks
The noise of trampling hoofs, and shakes
The solid earth, he thunders past,
Outpouring on the riven blast
His notes of warning, shrill and loud,
Through vapors rolling cloud on cloud,
In purple-bordered volumes; yea,
In storm and darkness, night and day,
Through mountain gorge or level way,
With tightening rein and might unspent,
And head erect in scorn of space,
Holds, neck-and-neck, with time a race,
Flame-girt across a continent.

II
Think not of danger, every wheel
Of all that clank and roll below,
Rang singing answers, steel for steel,
Beneath the hammer's testing blow:
And what, though fields go swirling round,
And backward swims the mazy ground,
So swift the herds seem standing still —
As scared they dash from hill to hill;
And though the brakes may grind to fire,
The gravel as they grip the tire,
And holding, strike a startling vein
Of tremor through the surging train,
The hand of him who guides the rein,
Is all controlling and intent:
Fear not, although the race you ride
Is on the whirlwind, side by side
With time across a continent.

Chance encounters change lives all the time. The details lie in the who, when, and where. J.P. and Harriett, known as Hattie, arrived in Washington, DC, by summer 1872. They had left the heartbreak and turmoil of the West — Illinois was still considered the West — and aimed for a fresh start on the bustling East Coast.

Irvine worked in the Bureau of Pensions, where he joined an army of clerks assembled to distribute payments to the country's sizable new population of Civil War veterans. The antebellum office employed 72 people, a number that grew to 1,500 by 1885.

Several notable writers spent their days as clerks in the capital. Walt Whitman in the Attorney General's office at the Department of Justice. John Burroughs at the Department of the Treasury.

Whitman and Burroughs became friends in the city, but both left in 1873, which allows for about a year of overlap with Irvine. I have found no evidence that proves they met one another, but the possibility is real.

Perhaps an encounter occurred at the mixing bowl that was the Metropolitan Hotel on Pennsylvania Avenue. The portico of the landmark building earned a reputation for visitors as diverse as Whitman, General Sam Houston, and Beau Hickman, a famous mooch and a subject of one of

Irvine's poems.

These names and others were part of a vibrant literary and social culture into which Irvine had stepped. This poem was printed in *The Capital*, which, along with *The Evening Star*, predated *The Washington Post*. Similar to "The Wooden Leg," this piece contains fanciful character names and traces a comical arc, though here to comment on the styles of the city.

A brace means a pair. Chignon is a coil of hair on the back of the head. Oroide is an alloy used for cheap gold jewelry. Pannier describes the part of the skirt around the hips, or the hoop that holds it.

A Brace of Canary Birds

The Male
T. Simmons Fitz Noodle is attached to a cane —
(That pun needs explaining, I mean as a friend of it) —
Of his love of a dear little, sweet little cane,
With the leg of a woman stuck tilt on the end of it.

T. Simmons Fitz Nood. wears a languishing air,
And a ring on his neckerchief, just for the tie of it;
In the middle he parts both his love and his hair
And the glass on his nose, with a string at the eye of it.

On the oroide chain of his watch there's a head
Of an owl or a gander, but a fig for the name of it,
Since but little it boots, as it serves in its stead
To emphasize his when comparing the brain of it.

Then his narrow-toed, oval-shaped, sled-runner
shoes,
His left little finger with the very long nail on it,
And his very long ears, and his barber-pole hose,
And the latest-cut coat, with a very brief tail on it.

Saying naught of his very cheap wit and his talk,
With its drive and slang, and billiards, and drink of
him,
And his women and conquests of virtue, and walk,
Is the make-up of Noodle, and just what I think of
him.

The Female
Miss Gussie Van Goosie is a delicate blonde
With a chignon that woos by the grace of the hang
of it,
Then add, if you will, to this beautiful blonde,
The hair on her intellect and the sweet bang of it.

Miss Gussie Van Goosie has a wasp of a waist

And the fullest of eyes, but so short is the breath of
her,
Since her liver is pinched and her lungs are
displaced
I'm afraid that tight lacing will soon be the death of
her.

But her pannier's not pinched — you can make up
your mind,
While she favors inflation as you'll see by the swing
of it,
While among its department of news you will find
A file of *The Capital* strung on the string of it.

Moreover, Miss Gussie takes arsenic, and paints,
Chews gum (on the sly) and she thinks you don't
know of it,
Laughs sweetly by note, flirts, waltzes and faints,
Wears a shoe with the heel but an inch from the toe
of it.

Then the puffings and bows, and the style of her
hat,
And Fannie, a poodle, the dear little pink of her,
And a spread-eagle fan and her trail, and all that
Is the make-up of Gussie, and just what I think of
her.

A familiar scene of modern-day gridlock unfolded in the nation's capital on May 30, 1873 — Decoration Day, what we now call Memorial Day. The roads, reported by the *Star*, "were thronged with . . . a jam of pedestrians, horsemen, and vehicles all the morning." Irvine would have traveled from his residence at 924 New York Avenue NW.

More than 10,000 spectators crowded the grounds at Arlington Cemetery for a lavish but somber celebration of the nation's defenders. A dispatch in *The New York Times* estimated 15,000. A letter published in Louisiana's *Donaldsonville Chief* pushed the number to 20,000.

Ornaments for adorning graves included wreaths, flowers, crosses, anchors, shields, and miniature American flags. "The decorations today were more elaborate than ever before . . . and everything done to add to the appearance of the silent city of the dead," the Star reported.

President Ulysses S. Grant and First Lady Julia headlined the ceremonies. Department secretaries of state, war, and treasury attended, as did Frederick Douglass. Songs and prayers opened the program, including one by Reverend T. De Witt Talmage.

"But let us bring no partisan feelings in this decoration of graves. In other years, in some places, demagogues have tried to make capital out of such gatherings, but I do not believe in bartering with the bones of our country's martyrs. They have done enough work."

Talmage built widespread renown with his oratory as the leader of the Central Presbyterian Church in Brooklyn, where he spent 25 years. Newspapers across the country carried his sermons. *The New York Times* reported that, with the sole exception of Henry Ward Beecher, Talmage "had a more widespread reputation than any other American preacher of the gospel."

He concluded his Arlington address with a stirring call.

"I offer you everlasting thanks in the name of a Union restored, of a government re-established and a race redeemed from servitude, so that from the time the sun rises in the eastern coast until it sets behind the Sierra Nevadas its burning eye cannot discover a single slave."

Like the other poets and writers in DC, I have found no proof that Irvine met Talmage. But a conversation between two speakers at a national event seems highly likely. It would not be their last encounter.

The thousands soon gathered at the Tomb of the Unknown Soldier, draped with garlands of evergreens. Irvine stepped up to read aloud the following poem under a clear sky and the heat of midday. At least two papers published all 111 lines: the May 30 edition of the *Star* and the June 13 edition of *The Monmouth Atlas*.

This remains Irvine's most noteworthy work both because of its content and the circumstances under which he presented it. Yet he chose not to include it in his book two decades later.

The more pressing question concerns why Irvine, still unknown himself, was selected for this role, a singular moment in his life that would cascade into new opportunities. Perhaps Whitman had been asked but passed for health complications from the stroke he'd suffered earlier in the year. A more likely scenario involves Irvine and the social temperament of the nation's capital. More than other American cities, DC thrives on connections.

What Irvine lacked in name recognition — none — he balanced with geography.

Kirkwood lies 150 miles from two critical Illinois elements. Traveling southeast leads you to Decatur, where the Grand Army of the Republic was founded in 1866. That veterans group established Decoration Day two years later. Traveling the same distance north puts you in the hills of Galena, where President Grant lived before he arrived in the Oval Office.

How Irvine finally received the invitation for a

turn at the podium that day remains unclear, but the potential contacts were in place. His next task required a memorable poem, which he delivered.

The themes and imagery of the Civil War appear in many of his lesser poems not included in this book, but those ideas and tinkerings find full maturity in this single piece, his most ambitious work.

The end of the first stanza echoes soldier and poet Theodore O'Hara's "Bivouac of the Dead." Four lines of that work are etched into one of the entrance arches to Arlington Cemetery. "On fame's eternal camping ground / their silent tents are spread, / And glory guards with solemn round, / the bivouac of the dead."

The beginning of the second stanza alludes to an ancient speech attributed to Pericles: "I speak not of that in which their remains are laid, but of that in which their glory survives . . . not only are they commemorated by columns and inscriptions in their own country, but in foreign lands there dwells also an unwritten memorial of them, graven not on stone but in the hearts of men."

The middle of the fourth stanza recalls Deuteronomy 34:6, when God buries Moses in the land of Moab, "but no man knows his burial place to this day."

The start of the sixth stanza invokes Psalm 39:

"Thou hast made my days as handbreadths, and my lifetime as nothing in Thy sight. Surely every man at his best is a mere breath."

Riven is a synonym for split. Ween means of the opinion. Tattoo here refers to the evening signal to call soldiers back to their quarters. Lay, in this sense, means a short lyric. A temporary camp is known as a bivouac. Eld means former times. A fen is an area of marsh, and a lea is an area of open grass or cropland. A short song with a refrain is called a roundelay, a word that originates from the French rondeau, *a specific poetic form like the sonnet or haiku.*

UNKNOWN

A sigh is as old as the primitive years
And a minor refrain as the song of the stars;
And the children of men were weary with tears,
E're sorrow was crowned in the kingdom of wars;
Yet, when the grim Harvester calls for his own,
And afar to the angels he carries a sheaf,
Our sickles we drop and away all alone
We hide in the shade of a sanctified grief;
Alone, with the poor stricken heart that is bowed,
Till at length it is quickened and breaks with its pain,
And weeps out its woe as a low brooding cloud
When riven with lightning its burden of rain.

But the sadness that lingers is softened, I ween,
And the vagueness of longing is tinged with delight,
Till the love that's remembered becomes as a dream,
Or a voice that is lost in the hush of the night,
But today we come forth, and in fancy review
The silent encampment here tenting about,
For it seems but a night since it beat the tattoo
When the pickets came in, and the lights were put out.
And the valiant are here; and the weak, and the strong;
The known, and unknown, and the army is Fame's
And the roll is a wonderful roll, and so long
That we weary of reading its dearest of names.

Unknown, did I say? Ah! none are unknown
Though strangers to us, and it may be to art;
Though engraven the baffled endeavor on stone —
The name is recorded in somebody's heart;
There's a brother somewhere bereft of a joy,
Or a sister, mayhap, of a brother's fond trust;
Or a father who grieves for his beautiful boy,
Here only a handful of fugitive dust;
Or a Rachel, lamenting the fruit of her womb,
With an anguish too sharp for the healings of time
For I have a brother asleep in the tomb

And the love of our mother I think is divine;
Or a child in its orphanage, knowing not yet,
Of a father enthralled to an absolute fate;
Or a widow, perchance, in her tearful regret,
Long watching and waiting alone at the gate.

And there's somebody, still, who is singing the lay:
"When Johnnie comes marching" to ne'er again
roam,
For hope is the same with the Blue and the Grey
But Johnnie — poor Johnnie — will never march
home.

Yes, the nameless are legion who come nevermore,
And these are but skirmishes bivouacked here,
Alas! they are scattered abroad the land o'er
As the leaves of the wood in the fall of the year
Ah! the Union is wide and they sleep as of eld
The prophet of God, in a Moabite plain,
In a sepulcher never by human beheld,
And angels alone is the funeral train:
They're hidden, I know, in the wilderness shades;
In coves, and lagoons, and fen-lands and leas;
In the plains of the palm, and the evergreen glades,
In forests of pine and the depth of the seas,
Away in the mountains, and lonely ravines,
In thickets, and wilds, where the wounded have
crept;

In the shadow of cliffs, on the margin of streams,
Where they perished alone, unnursed and unwept.
In the corners of fields, and old camping grounds:
By springs, and the windings of hoof-beaten roads;
By the hedges, and lanes, and by-ways and mounds,
On the skirting of creeks, and the flanking of fords;
In prisons and hospitals noisome and damp,
On the march, in all weather, in the day-time and night,
Of wounds and exposure, and the fevers of camp,
And the bullet, and sword, in the obstinate fight,
Oh! the story were sad, if the story were told
And the roll would be long were it mustered and called;
But neither, the wisdom of years can unfold,
And dear-hearted love will remain unappalled.
'Tis wisdom sufficient to know that they died —
A wonderful army — at home and afar —
That loyalty triumphed, and valor was tried
When the Union was racked in the thunders of war

To know that they died is a truth that reveals
The kinship of men to be more than a breath,
And a knowledge, baptized in affliction, that seals
The proof of a love that is stronger than death.
Then cease ye to mourn, and list unto reason —
For the way is not far to the white-tented land —

They will ne'er come to us, but ere a brief season
We'd deploy unto them at the word of command;
Away to the camp where the weary retreat,
Where toil is a stranger and war is unknown;
Where the roll is uncalled and the drums never
beat,
And the charge is unmade and the bugles unblown,
But the world they have left is a beautiful world,
And Freedom has gone from its manger of birth
And the angel of Peace with her pinions unfurled,
Is bearing the news through the glorified earth;
And the sword in its sheath, and the bayonet rust,
And the haversacks hang in the attics and halls;
And the rations remaining have mildewed to dust,
And the canteens are empty and hang on the walls;
And the North is extending a hand to the South
And the tides of their blood will again never ebb,
And the cannon is silent and over its mouth
The spider unfrightened is weaving her web.
Then their low-lying graves let us garland with
flowers
Full blown, and profound, and of manifold hue —
They are delicate gifts — these symbols of ours
And born of the heart, and the sun, and the dew;
And join, oh! ye minstrels, ye blithe-hearted
throng,
Dear blue-bird and robin your roundelays sing,
And thrushes, and bob-o-links tipsy with song,

For the dull ear of death may be quick when ye sing.
And ye, wooing winds blowing wildly and free,
And ye, of the crystalline army of stars
United in the hymn of the great jubilee,
At the crowning of peace and the ceasing of wars.

Although he couldn't foresee the effects of his time in DC, Irvine's three years set multiple springboards.

Capital newspapers printed his poems for new audiences. The most influential national magazines in the late 19th century — *Harper's* and *Scribner's* — published his work in subsequent years. Several of these poems became his most popular and were later collected into anthologies. And on a personal level, J.P. and Harriett welcomed the healthy baby Annabel Lee in 1873.

Irvine also entered the writing community, which included reading one of his poems at a so-called Literary Reunion hosted at the home of Horatio King. The man had served as Postmaster General prior to the Civil War and then worked as an attorney for many years in DC.

Reunion gatherings occurred on Saturday evenings in the winter and spring. The group began in 1870 and counted senators, judges, doctors, professors, clergy, and writers among its ranks — men and women. Their discussion topics would still resonate today; for example, a conversation about the coexistence of Darwinism and theology.

King opened one season with a speech, a kind of mission statement.

"For what do we live? Is it to retire within our

narrow sphere . . . [or] come out into the sunlight of social intercourse, of music, and of song? I confess it is with a degree of sadness that I look back toward boyhood and behold how much of my life has been absorbed by mere drudgery . . . . [Y]et we are resolved (are we not?) never in spirit to grow old . . ."

English professor emeritus James Doyle, of Wilfrid Laurier University, has noted that U.S. magazines thrived after the Civil War until the turn of the century for reasons as varied as a shortage of paper suitable for books and higher literacy rates. Yet, "typical magazine poetry was relentlessly traditional" and churned out by writers "generally committed to an imitative and dogmatic conception of poetry."

Irvine fits that mold for plenty of his pieces, especially early in his life. And rightly so. Publication meant payment, even if it also meant tired rhyme schemes and worn patterns of traditional meter. As the romanticism gave way to realism, poets began experimenting and producing work that we now regard as modern genius. The poem below was published in 1866, but it shows one of the few instances where Irvine progresses into complete free verse.

Stanza XIII references Isaiah 2:4. "They will beat their swords into plowshares and their spears into pruning hooks. Nation will not take up sword against nation, nor will they train for war anymore."

Euphony means a pleasing sound. Kirkyard is a Scottish term for a church cemetery.

THE NEW YEAR

PRELUDE

To Him whose mercies fell around
My pathway day by day,
As thither to the ferry bound,
I plod my erring way,
I gladly lift my soul and sing
A hymn to Pilgrim time,
Though old its euphony, I'll sing
On silver bells of rhyme,
Full sounding flow the major tones
In tranquil harmony,
And like the ocean's troubled moans
Be sorrow's minor key;
For right and left our fates have run
Between our hopes and fears,
As shadows alternate with sun,
So pass the dappled years.

GONE

He has gone beyond the River,
Through the valley chill and dark,
With his twelve erratic children,
A snow-haired Patriarch

Yet ere his crossing over,
Peace from out her horn had poured
Her lavish balm of Gilead
Through the gashes of the sword.

Cut deep in fearful struggle
On the carnage field, alas!
Where the blood of martyred heroes
Turned to gore upon the grass.

Well, these were times of trouble;
And we never shall forget
Our agony and tossings,
Through nights of bloody sweat.

But a telegram at morning
Our pent up tears unsealed;
"In their army blankets shrouded"
"They were buried on the field!"

Then came the tender spring time,
With clover nooks and birds,
To woo away our grieving,
Like a Nun's consoling words.

And doves came to our windows
With their plucks of olive spray;
And the roll of battle thunders
Grew fainter day by day.

Then, as a flash of lightning,
From the azure heavens sent,
Came the news that smote us speechless —
Our murdered President!

We did not weep; the flood gates
Of our souls were choked with grief;
We could only grieve in spirit,
We so loved our murdered chief.

At length the flood gates bursted,
And our sorrow deluged forth;
Then we rose and swore revenge,
And we well fulfilled the oath.

Then Spring to Summer glided
Flooding fields with amber grain,
Healing o'er the scars of battle,

With the sunshine and the rain.
And the soldier, turned to farmer,
[illegible]
And the [illegible]
Now bound the golden sheaves

And the swords of haughty Rebels,
By the sweat of manly brows,
Were beaten into pruning hooks
And shares for Yankee plows

To break the wilds where
From blood hounds lay concealed,
The war trail worn and trodden
To a thrifty cotton field.

Ho! Southward! men of action,
With your Bibles and your looms;
Go, chase away the darkness
From the land of Rebel tombs.

Ho! Southward! singing anthems
To Him whose mercies gave
The year foretold by prophets,
A land without a slave!

Forward and backward, stand I on the juts
Of time and look; somewhat I've wandered

Through the Past, foot-sore, scrambling up its
steeps,
And sauntering here and there, sometimes in
woods
And wilderness, [illegible]
The farm, through town and through-fares where
trade
And traffic roar and babel all day long.
In passing thus I've read the signs,
And numbers on the doors, and dates engraved
In marble in the Kirk-yards far and wide,
The mile-stones every one I've numbered
In my strolls, and kept a note of all the landmarks,
You see I'm full familiar with the little
Corner of my life, and like the Hebrew King
Have found that all is vanity,
Hence I'm weary of the Past, and wish
To know no more.

The far Beyond —
I seem to see its castles built of air;
I seem to hear a sweet voice singing,
"Come this way," Beware! the rainbow and
Bag of gold no mortal e'er hath gained.
I go. Of course my destiny lies there,
But how uncertain to this timid mind,
To Him alone who doeth all things well,

Let's give our hand, and uncomplaining go
As He shall thither lead.

The stump of the incomplete Washington Monument loomed for decades as the most recognizable, and perhaps most reviled, sight in the capital. Construction began in 1848, funded by the Washington National Monument Society. In a move fitting for DC, competing politics invaded the private society's governing board, and the group went bankrupt by 1854. So the stone structure sat like a chimney without a house for more than twenty years.

The title of the following poem refers to 1 Samuel 4:21, where the Philistines trounce the troops of Israel. A woman gives birth to a son she names Ichabod because "the glory has departed from Israel."

Irvine expanded his criticism from this poem into a much longer work called "Concerning Washington and His Monument." The booklet was illustrated by Alfred Downing and published in 1875. Lady Liberty releases an eagle and points to a sky full of vultures on the cover. The dark birds swarm a tree with contribution boxes attached to the trunk, and several birds pull money from slots.

The Evening Star reviewed that chapbook: "Mr. Irvine has brought his very decided poetical abilities to the patriotic work of showing up with sarcastic point the national disgrace involved in the unfinished condition of the Washington

Monument."

Congress took control of funding the iconic obelisk in 1876. The length of time that had passed forced masons to use stone from quarries other than the original, and the slight color difference persists today. With consistent public funding, construction finally finished in 1884.

Inveigle means to persuade by deception or flattery. Derrick, often used now in reference to oil wells, indicates a crane.

ICHABOD

It is far from my wish to inveigle
Fond faith, from top-loftical things,
But a length of the tail of the eagle,
Should, in short, be curtailed from his wings.

For soaring, he alights (without joking)
On the monument's top — as you know —
And because it's unfinished, sits croaking
"Nevermore," like the Raven of Poe!

Since truth is the prophecy spoken,
Then the typical bird who can blame?
For the pledge of the nation is broken,
And her gratitude branded with shame.

Like the castle confounded at Babel,
So it stands a derisive reproof,
With a weather-warped, clap-boarded gable,
And a derrick-like thing on the roof.

And crumbling, the ill-tempered mortar,
Is dusting the cob-webs and bats,
While the inner walls make a safe quarter,
For stampeded neighborhood rats.

Better then on the door stick a knob
That will lock with a bolt, and thereon,
As of old, write the word "Ichabod"
Which means that the glory has gone.

Spending time in a cosmopolitan hub on the eastern seaboard meant Irvine had experienced a vast swath of the country — from Niagara Falls and DC to major urban centers in the Midwest to the Rocky Mountains. There's a considerable chance he visited his close friends, the Allens, in California. Such travel granted Irvine remarkable perspective as poetic preferences continued to push away from romanticism and toward realism. As realism took hold, another movement developed.

New England had already established its regional flavor by the early to mid 19th century, but broad adoption of regionalism within the realist framework happened after the Civil War. Anne Rowe, former English professor and dean at Florida State University, has argued that regionalism existed as a form of early nostalgia after the war, a conflict almost exclusively fought on the premise of national versus regional priorities. Others have insisted that regionalism served an important function by presenting contemporary chronicles of a complex — but unified — country.

An eminent literary critic of the time, William Dean Howells, asserted that American writing didn't begin until after the war. "[A]s soon as the country began to feel its life in every limb with the coming of peace, it began to speak in the varying accents of all the different sections — North, East, South, West, and Farthest West; but not before that time."

Along with all the advantages the capital produced for Irvine's life, the disquieting regularity of tragedy also met the family on the coast. Sometime shortly after Annabel's birth, Harriett suffered a stroke. She lived as an invalid for 35 years before her death in 1908 from the effects of paralysis.

Irvine led his stricken wife and young daughter back west by summer 1875. Local news briefs that document the social comings and goings of Irvine and his friends in Kirkwood never mention Harriett, a woman stuck between the sleep and death depicted in this poem.

The theme resembles "Two Towns," but this piece goes further to demonstrate Irvine's range. He so often incorporated faith-based references, but he also anthropomorphized abstract concepts like time, death, and weather. He pulled from mythology and ancient Greco-Roman literature. He criticized policies and politics. None of these examples surface in Irvine's lone book.

Ween means of the opinion.

TWO TAVERNS

On the river slopes I tarry,
Where the flakes of clover grow,
As moon beams o'er the waters
Their silver pontoons throw
When all my thoughts a-rambling,
Troop over to and fro.

To southward thrice a furlong
On airy-sandaled feet;
Through the care-encumbered city,
Through the toil-beleaguered street,
Now, like the sea from tempest,
In the holy calm of sleep.

Then northward, light as fairies
In their dance of sylvan rounds,
To the clumps of thrifty maple
On yonder burial grounds,
Where supple feet grow heavy
Amid the crowded mounds.

So come, my musing members
So weary grown ye seem;
Come, sit down amid the clover,
My Paradise, I ween;

Come, nestle in my bosom,
My beloved, while we dream.

And so they came and nestled,
And we dreamed, in visions sweet,
That Sleep and Death kept taverns
On either side the street;
That one kept transient lodgers
And gave them wine and meat.

And the other, entertainment
For comers night and day,
Whether straggling in at evening,
Or morning's twilight gray,
Through the doorway wreathed with cypress,
But they never went away.

PRAIRIE HYMNS

The level horizons of Illinois welcomed Irvine, but his world had tilted. The decade and a half between his return and the publication of *The Green Leaf and the Gray* all but silenced his printed record. A few poems and letters appeared in local newspapers, but the scarcity resembled his family's arrival in the west, when "the cabins were still few and far between, and not a human habitation to be seen" between the Irvine homestead and Monmouth.

Perhaps Harriett's condition after the stroke required too much attention to leave room for creative thoughts. His own health problems might have caused difficulties as well. Moreover, the local newspaper tendencies had changed. Whereas they printed multiple poems in each weekly issue during the 1860s and 1870s, they printed that many in a month by the 1880s. Then, the poems were often reprints from major monthly magazines.

Yet Irvine still wrote, even if he didn't publish

much. For instance, his poem about the demise of Jo Leeper, who died in 1888.

The 1880 census listed Irvine's official occupation as a newspaper editor, an indisputable fact given that he performed the duties of census enumerator that year. He filled out the federal documents, which left pages of samples to examine his handwriting and signature.

However, I don't know at which of the dozen or so Warren County newspapers Irvine worked. Microfilm copies and other traces don't survive from most of these long-gone publications. Irvine is not listed in the masthead of the Monmouth papers, but he might have served as the Kirkwood correspondent. Both Monmouth papers ran columns with news from surrounding communities, but none of these regular contributions carried bylines. The link: Irvine's daughter Annabel often assumed correspondent duties when the normal writer traveled, indicated by a short note before an extended trip.

Irvine reintegrated himself into the area where he grew up in other ways. The 1880 census also indicated that he owned a small farm plot with a half-acre of Irish potatoes and a one-acre apple orchard of 20 trees. His father and brother Robert farmed more extensively.

As one of the earliest families in the area, the

Irvines participated in the Old Settlers' Association. Locals in Warren County and neighboring Henderson County created the group in 1873 to celebrate frontier life and the steadfast people who committed to settling western Illinois.

Irvine read this poem at one of the annual pioneer picnics. On first glance, the romantic overtones seep through, but he's examining the idealistic viewpoint memory creates. The text fits firmly in the regionalism movement, but not by typical standards. He doesn't qualify as a regionalist in the common use of local dialects, but rather by how he applies detailed description to build a sense of place — the West, or as the country progressed in that direction, the Midwest.

A mow is a place, often a barn, where farmers stored hay or grain. A pucker-string is a drawstring. Burthen is an archaic form of burden. Isaiah 62:4 introduces Beulah, an ideal land that signifies marriage to God.

RHYMES OF THE FARM

No wonder one grows old so fast,
The hours unreckoned run;
A day flies like a shuttle thrown
Across from sun to sun.
Unceasingly the seasons glide
Within their courses ranged:

The world keeps spinning round and round.
And we alone are changed.

Aye, changed, though scarce because of years
That swiftly come and go;
The white flecks sprinkled in our beards
Are not all winter's snow;
'Tis not the weight of time alone
That leaves us bent and lame,
But burthens early borne beyond
The strength of mortal frame.

God help the shoulders that grow round
From toil because of need,
But not the back that bends beneath
A load of selfish greed;
God wipe the sweat from honest brows
That faint before the noon;
God pity us, it is not strange
We all grow old so soon.

The slow, dull drag behind the plow,
From twilight in the morn,
Till evening falls and darkens out
The long rows of the corn;
The broiling sun of harvest fields,
The stifling heat of mows,
The endless chores about the barns,

The drudge of milking cows —

Especially when days are bad,
And "Brindle" sends her tail
Kerslap across a fellow's face,
And over-kicks the pail!
It's pleasant too, to race a hog
Around and 'round a lot
Some twenty times right past the hole
Wherein the critter got!

To have a calf you're weaning ram
Its head — in wanton sport —
Into the milk above the eyes,
And then to give a snort!
To set a hen on fancy eggs
That cost a fancy price,
And have them hatch only to die
From cholera and lice!

To bet your money on a colt
You've trained to trot, to find
Him breaking down the homeward stretch
A half a mile behind;
To pet a lamb and have it butt
Your breath out when it grows;
To proffer seed of good intent
And reap a crop of woes.

All tend to shorten and to pull
The pucker-string of time,
And set the wrinkles round the eyes
Before a body's prime.
Work, work from early morn to night
Or weeds will surely grow,
There is no use to drop the seed
Unless you use the hoe.

The farm is not a playing ground,
The soil will only yield
The sheaf and cluster to the hand
That tills aright the field.
And though the plow-share never rusts
The furrows have no end,
Ere long the brow will cease to swear
The back will cease to bend.

As after toil comes recompense,
And bliss comes after pain,
It is the darkest cloud that pours
The fullest founts of rain.
'Tis but the story as of old,
Work, only trusting Him,
Hold out the empty cup and God
Will fill it to the brim.

So with the years come younger hands
To lift the burthen down;
And give the dear old folks a rest
By moving them to town,
Where every week they visit them
With cheer and kindly words,
And baskets filled with goodly things,
The best the farm affords.

Beneath the maples tilted back,
Adrowse in easy chairs —
Their silver-threaded temples fanned
With soft autumnal airs —
They turn in fondness to the past —
Forgetful of its ills —
The distance seems not half so long
Nor half so rough the hills.

For lo, the great green goodly land
Of yore comes into view;
Again the distant groves are robed
Like isles in purple hue;
Once more the grand old prairies sweep,
And roll, and flash and change,
As rolls a sapphire sea, till lost
Beyond the boundless range.

Once more the cattle graze at will,
The deer in tandem run;
The uncovered quail in coveys flock
Unscared of net or gun;
And as in morns of early spring,
When dews the grasses pearled,
Again the prairie chickens belt
With mellow beams the world.

Earth held no land so beautiful,
No clime so sweet with song;
No wonder memory backward strays
And loves to cling so long.
And yet one forward glance in faith,
One look with steadfast eyes
And lo, amid the purple hills
The vale of Beulah lies;

A land that joins just this side heaven,
Of one perpetual spring,
And, aye, so near the golden gates
You hear the angels sing;
A land wherein your hurts are healed
Of earth that so oppressed —
A claim of everlasting love
And everlasting rest.

The United States has always represented "a democratic West in opposition to an aristocratic East," according to *The Cambridge History of English and American Literature*. That dichotomy proved itself, whether in the colonies versus England, or Chicago versus New York City, or California versus Kansas City.

An initial split in literary sensibilities happened between the Atlantic seaboard and everything west. The Cambridge history compared the "fidelity to a noble tradition" and "approved types of beauty" on the coast to the "fidelity to experience" and "vitality of utterance" in the lands beyond sight of the waves.

Regionalism gained strength within the realism movement, and Irvine could claim allegiance to the area where he spent most of his life. Monmouth College's student newspaper, *The Annex*, wrote, "Mr. Irvine belongs to Warren [sic] county and the west, and has long been recognized as occupying a front rank . . ."

However, Irvine held a charmed position. His words welled from a mind rooted in the west, yet he had mingled with the culture centers across the country. Several of the poems in this section secured Irvine's notoriety for his skillful depictions of nature. His most influential geographic peers noticed.

James Newton Matthews, the "Poet of the Prairie," and James Whitcomb Riley, "The Hoosier Poet," helped organize the first literary society beyond the Appalachian Mountains.

The Western Association of Writers lasted about 20 years after its founding in 1886. The group concentrated around Indiana but included officers representing states as far as Montana and Colorado. Annual meetings brought writers together for several days of readings, discussions, and social festivities.

Newspapers in the region hailed the WAW: "[I]n view of the vigorous growth of a distinctive literature of the West, and the importance of upholding its excellence and dignity, and improving the welfare of its professional workers this association is an urgent need."

In early 1891, Matthews wrote to Riley: "I have lately made the acquaintance of a poet of no 'middle flight.' . . . [Irvine has] hobnobbed with the literary magnates of the East. . . . He is showing considerable interest in our Writers' Association, and I shall collar him and bring him to our next meeting."

WAW documents and minutes show that Irvine never presented a poem as part of an official program, but that fact does not preclude his possible attendance. He later inscribed a copy of

his book, with his best wishes, to "a brother singer"
— Dr. James Newton Matthews.

    A suppliant person makes a plea to an authority
figure. Mullein is a common weed that grows yellow
flowers on tall spikes of vegetation, sometimes up to 10
feet. A wain is a wagon or cart. Anon means shortly.

SUMMER DROUGHT

When winter came the land was lean and sere:
There fell no snow, and oft from wild and field
In famished tameness came the drooping deer,
And licked the waste about the troughs congealed.

And though at spring we plowed and proffered
seed,
It lay ungermed, a pillage for the birds:
And unto one low dam, in urgent need,
We daily drove the suppliant, lowing herds.

But now the fields to barren waste have run,
The dam a pool of oozing greenery lies,
Where knots of gnats hang reeling in the sun
Till early dusk, when tilt the dragonflies.

All night the craw-fish deepens out her wells,
As shows the clay that freshly curbs them round;

And many a random upheaved tunnel tells
Where ran the mole across the fallow ground.

But ah! the stone-dumb dullness of the dawn,
When e'en the cocks too listless are to crow,
And lies the world as from all life withdrawn,
Unheeding and outworn and swooning low!

There is no dew on any greenness shed,
The hard-baked earth is cracked across the walks;
The very burrs in stunted clumps are dead
And mullein leaves drop withered from the stalks.

Yet, ere the noon, as brass the heaven turns,
The cruel sun smites with unerring aim,
The sight and touch of all things blinds and burns,
And bare, hot hills seem shimmering into flame!

On either side the shoe-deep dusted lane
The meager wisps of fennel scorch to wire;
Slow lags a team that drags an empty wain,
And, creaking dry, a wheel runs off its tire.

No flock upon the naked pasture feeds,
No blithesome bob-white whistles from the fence.
A gust runs crackling through the brittle weeds,
And then the heat still waxes more intense.

On outspread wings a hawk, far poised on high,
Quick swooping screams, and then is heard no
more:
The strident shrilling of a locust nigh
Breaks forth, and dies in silence as before.

No transient cloud o'erskims with flakes of shade
The landscape hazed in dizzy gleams of heat;
A dove's wing glances like a parried blade,
And western walls the beams in torrents beat.

So burning low, and lower still the sun,
In fierce white fervor, sinks anon from sight,
And so the dread, despairing day is done,
And dumbly broods again the haggard night.

In his 1891 letter, Matthews also told Riley that Irvine, whose "whole soul is baptized to poetry," would release a book that year.

Irvine had visited Chicago the previous December to arrange for publication. He worked with the W.B. Conkey Company and persisted through several delays due to the publisher's other production schedules.

The Monmouth Daily Review reported that the book's first shipment of 300 copies arrived on May 28, "and in a very short space of time they were all gone." He received a second edition in July and a third round in December. He published *The Green Leaf and the Gray* with his own money and sold the books for $1.

In September, Irvine received a letter from New York City. The poet Edmund Stedman sent congratulations. Stedman, another Whitman connection, made his name as a critic and editor of some of the most influential poetry anthologies at that time. Although he and Whitman were acquaintances, Stedman enjoyed a much deeper friendship with William Dean Howells.

Stedman probably passed along a recommendation to his friend, who reviewed the book a few months later in *Harper's*. Howells, a widely known literary critic, wrote the Editor's Study column for the magazine and also worked as an editor for more than a decade at *The Atlantic*.

"There is great inequality in his performance ... and yet two or three of the descriptive pieces are as good landscape art in the modern sort as we could well find." Among those, Howells included this poem and the previous one. The *Chicago Tribune* also marked this poem as one of Irvine's best and called it "nearly pure gold." And the personal papers of Henry Wadsworth Longfellow contained a newsprint clipping of the poem.

INDIAN SUMMER

At last the toil encumbered days are over,
And airs of noon are mellow as the morn;
The blooms are brown upon the seeding clover,
And brown the silks that plume the ripening corn.

All sounds are hushed of reaping and of mowing;
The winds are low; the waters lie uncurled;
Nor thistle-down nor gossamer is flowing,
So lull'd in languid indolence the world.

And mute the farms along the purple valley,
The full barns muffled to the beams with sheaves;
You hear no more the noisy rout and rally
Amongst the tenant-masons of the eaves.

A single quail, upstarting from the stubble,
Darts whirring past and quick alighting down
Is lost, as breaks and disappears a bubble,
Amid the covert of the leafy brown.

The upland glades are flecked afar in dapples
By flocks of lambs a-gambol from the fold;
The orchards bend beneath the weight of apples,
And groves are bright in crimson and in gold.

But hark! I hear the pheasant's muffled drumming,
The water murmur from a distant dell;
A drowsy bee in mazy tangles humming;
The far, faint tinkling tenor of a bell.

And now from yonder beech trunk sheer and
sterile,
The rat-tat-tat of the wood-pecker's bill;
The sharp staccato barking of a squirrel,
A dropping nut, and all again is still.

September 1891 brought not only Stedman's letter but also a substantial half-column book review in the *Chicago Tribune*.

"Mr. Irvine's gift of melody is indeed remarkable, and . . . [he] adds a sense of color and a faculty of sympathetic observation which have served him well." The review tabbed several poems worthy of wide readership, and compared much of Irvine's work in the book to Alfred Lord Tennyson, "not only in form and melody but by reason of a certain vague suggestiveness."

The comparison is flattering but myopic. The strengths in the comprehensive body of Irvine's work, as affirmed in this book, don't begin to shine through in the selections he published in *The Green Leaf and the Gray*.

The book's faults balanced the *Tribune's* commendations.

"We have been glad to praise Mr. Irvine's work, and to recognize the vein of genuine poetry which is his, for as a Western man he has a claim of his own upon our sympathies. At the same time we must not convey the impression that Mr. Irvine is a finished writer. The motive of many of his poems is slight — too slight for the beauty of the execution."

The *Tribune* called Irvine a master of the iambic form, but accomplished prosody is not necessarily invigorating poetry. Skillful and stiff ranks below raw and evocative, the latter shining through in this poem. John Burroughs, the writer-naturalist friend of Whitman's, thought well enough of this poem and the previous two to include them in his 1901 anthology *Songs of Nature*.

Burroughs wrote that the collection represented "my judgment of the best Nature poems at my disposal in the language . . . true to the reality without and to the emotion within."

A mow is a place, often a barn, where farmers stored hay or grain.

An August Afternoon On the Farm

In stifling mows the men became oppressed,
And hastened forth hard breathing and o'rcome;
The hatching hen stood panting in her nest,
The sick earth swooned in languor and was dumb.

The dust-dull'd crickets lay in heedless ease
Of trampling hoofs along the beaten drives,
And from the fields the home-returning bees,
Limp wing'd and tired, lit short before their hives.

The drooping dog moped aimlessly around;
Lop'd down, got up, snapt at the gnats; in pits

Knee deep, the tethered horses stamped the
ground,
And switched at bot-flies dabbing yellow nits.

With heads held prone the sheep in huddles stood
Through fear of gads — the lambs, too, ceased to
romp;
The cows were wise to seek the covert wood,
Or belly deep stand hidden in the swamp.

So dragged the day, but when the dusk grew deep
The stagnant heat increased; we lit no light,
But sat out-doors, too faint and sick for sleep;
Such was the stupor of that August night.

All the literary praise in the world wouldn't stem the workload of caring for a family and a small farm. Annabel contracted the measles in early 1891, but she rallied to health. "Miss Annabel Irvine canvassed Biggsville yesterday with her father's book of poems and met with unusually good success in taking orders for this already popular book."

Between her mother's long-ago painting skills and her father's writing abilities, Annabel tended toward the latter. She participated in literary programs at school and eventually took over as the full-time correspondent for the Kirkwood news column in *The Monmouth Daily Review*. Irvine celebrated her younger days with this poem, one that the *Tribune* specifically applauded.

Both writers probably joined the trainload of people from Kirkwood who rode to Monmouth in February 1892 to hear a noted orator. Irvine doubtfully would have passed on the chance to introduce his daughter — the two men had spoken in front of President Grant a few months before Annabel's birth. Rev. T. De Witt Talmage's national notoriety had continued to increase during the intervening years. Irvine's comparably less so.

Artless means natural and simple. Limpid describes something clear.

AT THE PASTURE BARS

Returning lonely from the field,
She met me at the pasture bars;
The moon was like a golden shield,
The firmament was lit with stars.

As morning dawn her face was mild,
As evening, so her limpid eyes
God never gave a sweeter child
For weary man to idolize.

So winsome seemed her artless mirth,
Her soft caress and ardent kiss;
I thought of all delights of earth
The angels surely covet this.

I know they mean to do no ill,
But whom they love they lure away;
Good angels, love her as ye will,
But leave her with me while I stay.

Just as she is, for I would set
The hand of time behind an hour,
If that would stay a little yet
The bud from blooming to the flower.

But when at length we homeward went,
The fragrant azure shone so clear,
The great familiar firmament,
I thought, had never seemed so near.

So near, the moon above the trees
An airy globe of silver swung;
And in the dewy tops of these
The stars in mellow clusters hung.

So near, that I could scarce forego
The thought that one who longing waits,
Might hear them singing sweet and low,
Of love beyond the golden gates.

Irvine does not clear the bar to become a literary figure of worldwide or even national prominence. We should consider his place as a significant minor figure in American poetry, particularly of the West.

This poem describes the vast, blank prairie and offers an example on multiple levels that supports the conclusion in *The Cambridge History of English and American Literature*. "It was perhaps a certain bareness in Middle Western life, lacking both the longer memories of the Atlantic States and the splendid golden expectations of California, that thus early established in the upper Mississippi valley the realistic tradition . . ."

Howells, an astute man and an advocate for realism over romanticism, could see the literary landscape expanding beyond the tidy enclaves of the East Coast. His 1892 review of Irvine's book in *Harper's* included several other works.

"They bear witness to the truth of the Study's theory that in 'this fair land,' as the politicians call it, there is properly no literary centre. . . . [O]ne might argue that the centre of poetry, if we have any, was now, like the centre of population, far beyond the [sic] Alleghanies. . . .

"[U]nless something is done to bring up the worn-out fields of thought at the East by the lavish use of fertilizers, or a new system of cultivation, the future is sure to be anxiously awaited there. . . .

"[T]he Western product will have its own flavor; and no watering-pot process will give us the color and perfume of Mr. Riley's *Old-fashioned Roses,* grown in the open air, and fanned by the breath of the prairies."

In the estimation of Howells, the kind of writers who would lead the change from beyond the mountains included Riley but not Irvine or any other authors reviewed in that column.

"All or nearly all of these books bear to the experienced eye the sad evidences of having been published by or for the authors; and the reader must not infer a pecuniary boom in poetry from their appearance."

Howells correctly interpreted *The Green Leaf and the Gray* as self-published. That fact diminishes the likelihood Irvine worked with someone to select and shape the content. Writers need editors. A capable editor might have suggested that Irvine scrap the biographical tales and focus on poems that transcended common rhyme. Or an editor would have worked with the author to elevate the writing in those poems that lacked. But one book does not make the man.

A WINTER MORNING STILL LIFE

You have seen a winter morning,
The horizon dull and low,
When the earth and all belonging
Lay a level waste of snow.
In the drear and empty distance
There was naught of all we knew,
Save the gaunt and naked poplars
To arrest the wand'ring view.
It was as a stretch of desert
With no sign of life thereon —
The familiar hills and hollows
And the fields and fences gone;
Every road and lane and by-way,
Far and near were blotted out,
Hushed the sound of bells and silent
Were the huntsman's gun and shout;
E'en the axes of the choppers
Were unheard amid the wood,
And in drifts the horse of iron,
With his train imprisoned stood.
Save but once across the heavens,
When there flew a single crow,
Not a motion broke the blankness
Of the muffled world of snow.

The criticisms of Irvine's book hold true. In short, Irvine did not reliably expand beyond himself. Such a failure blights mediocre poets everywhere — to, for any number of reasons, not leap across the chasm from personal particularities to expansive truths.

Much of *The Green Leaf and the Gray* contained trivial observations or ethnographic poems written about friends and family. The *Chicago Tribune* admonished that "their interest is purely personal, and their artistic value is not high." A perfect example is "A Golden Wedding," nothing more than a poetic narrative of Irvine's parents and siblings.

Like any writer, Irvine didn't produce noteworthy work each time he touched paper. However, his lines that did meet this standard deserve more widespread recognition. Authentic scenes carried his nature poetry, and the Civil War poems often excelled in touching universal chords.

Even if his exceptional poems numbered just a few, those words remain important in the intellectual context of the Midwest in America's Gilded Age. Irvine contributed as part of the literary bedrock that would reach its height after the turn of the 20th century with the likes of Carl Sandburg, Edgar Lee Masters, and Harriet Monroe, who founded the groundbreaking *Poetry* magazine in 1912.

Irvine died at his cottage in Kirkwood, within sight of his eternal home, early on the morning of October 24, 1892. During the night, he uttered phrases like "Receive my spirit, oh God," and "Nearer, my God, to thee."

David, Jane, Robert, and J.P. all died between 1890 and 1896, the year Annabel married William Brown. The couple stayed in Illinois for several years before they moved to Long Beach, California, where they lived a mile and a half from the Pacific Ocean. Sara Jane, still unmarried and the last of Irvine siblings, lived with the Browns. Whether J.P.'s personal papers arrived on the West Coast remains unknown.

A coulter is the vertical blade on a plow. Aurora is the Roman goddess of dawn.

THE FARMER

I
Hail! Farmer, hail your station high,
I love the hand of honest toil,
Come, yoke the cattle — speed the plow
And turn the rich productive soil;
File the coulter sharp and keen,
Smoothly cut the stubble through,
Straightly guide the oaken beam,

Draw the furrow deep and true.
I love to watch your honest hand
Though clumsy, rough and weather-tanned,
Display its skillful art;
The master of a noble trade,
The highest in superior grade,
The index of the heart.

II
And now the fields in rustling corn,
In wheat and bearded rye,
In silken ears and yellow tops
Proclaim the harvest nigh;
Aurora peeps — the reaper's out,
The binder comes — they roll their sleeves
And soon their hands bestud the fields
With sturdy shocks of golden sheaves.
Come see, come see his honest hand
Though clumsy, rough and weather-tanned,
Display its skillful art;
The master of a noble trade,
The highest in superior grade,
The index of the heart.

III
The meadows now in wavy green
And velvet robes inviting, stand
And nod their plumage in the breeze,

Prepared to greet the farmer's hand;
He comes — he whets his glittering scythe,
In measured strokes he cuts his way,
And leaves behind a shaven lawn
And heavy swaths of scented hay.
From year to year his honest hand
Though clumsy, rough and weather-tanned,
Display its skillful art;
The master of a noble trade,
The highest in superior grade,
The index of the heart.

IV
But then I knew a farmer old,
Whose name is Time — he farms the brow;
He draws his furrows down the cheeks
And deeply runs his constant plow;
He ceases not for Winter's storms,
Nor heeds its snows nor chilly breath,
But ceaseless works Old Farmer Time
To fit us for the reaper Death.
Then let us mark his ruthless hand
Though very old and weather-tanned,
Display its magic art;
And be prepared to run and meet
And bow beneath the reaper's feet,
And yield this mortal part.

V

Because his sickle's sharp and keen,
And daily reaps with giant sway;
It touches, and like withered leaves
We fall and pass unknown away;
If bound in sheaves, he does it not,
If garnered up, 'tis not by him,
He reaps the flowers and bearded grain
But ceases not to gather in.
Then let us mark Time's ruthless hand,
Though very old and weather-tanned,
Display its magic art;
And be prepared to run and meet
And bow beneath the reaper's feet,
And yield this mortal part.

AFTERWORD

Amid my internet trolling and microfilm spinning, I found several mentions of poems whose full text I haven't (yet) found.

A note in *Publisher's Circular* in 1860 referenced a book of fiction called *Tales of a Tatler*, by J.P. Irvine. I'm not sure this is the same person.

A short announcement in the *National Republican* in 1873 introduced Irvine's new project of writing about the journalists of Washington, DC. "As a poet Mr. Irvine has earned a well-deserved prominence, and it is not at all strange that he should now turn his attention to new and inexhaustibly poetical subjects."

His obituaries indicated that he had finished "Quatrains of the Months and the Seasons," though the newspapers never specify whether that is a single poem or a new book.

Other pieces surely lurk in the microfilm of newspapers or magazines that have not met digitization. For instance, how could a person raised in a small town on the western edge of American civilization — the first telephone in Kirkwood arrived in May 1878 — later spend time in the nation's capital and not feel compelled to write more about the city? I've only found a few poems on that topic.

The best hope for answers, especially in unpublished form, lies in a collection of personal papers that might not exist today. Nevertheless, assuming someone saved his documents and unfinished works after his death, the following possibilities apply.

SCENARIO 1: He left them to a local public institution.

None of the suspected libraries or colleges in Illinois have Irvine's papers, though plenty of basements, attics, and storage rooms still hold potential.

SCENARIO 2: He left them to his mother.

Jane died in 1893, less than a year after J.P. If this scenario were true, the papers should proceed down the family line.

SCENARIO 3: He left them to his wife.

Harriet's condition after the stroke likely eliminated her eligibility for safeguarding Irvine's artifacts. Two of her siblings survived after her death in 1908, but brother R.W. Magennis lived in Topeka, Kansas, and sister Margaret Dixon lived in Jefferson, Iowa. Irvine's papers shouldn't have found their way so far afield when other family lived much closer.

SCENARIO 4: He left them to one of his siblings and their children.

Robert never married and died suddenly in 1896 in Kirkwood. He was reading a newspaper. Sara didn't marry either, and she died in 1927 after living her last years in California with her only niece.

SCENARIO 5: He left them to his daughter.

Annabel lived in Long Beach for more than thirty years with her husband. He died in 1941, and she died in 1949. California presents the best case for harboring any Irvine documents, but census reports never listed children for the couple.

VERDICT: Nobody in the Irvine line survives today, and the papers of this poet are, like he once was, lost. For now.

SOURCES

My research included census reports, cemetery visits, church records, Civil War documents and histories, vital records in county courthouses and online databases, county plat books, city directories, the archived papers of the Western Writers Association, a copy of *The Green Leaf and the Gray* signed by Sara Jane, and 20,000 pages of newspaper microfilm and digitized scans.

Sources for quotes aren't always referenced to streamline the narrative flow. Here's a full list of quoted periodicals, not italicized so you can actually read them: The Monmouth Atlas, The Monmouth Review, The Monmouth Daily Review, The Winnebago Chief, Winnebago County Chief, The Evening Star, The New York Times, The Annex, Chicago Tribune, and Harper's.

And the entries for specific works quoted in the book, aside from the *Bible*:

Monmouth College Oracle, souvenir edition, May 30, 1911

The History of the Thirty-Sixth Regiment Illinois Volunteers During the War of the Rebellion, L. G. Bennett and William M. Haigh, 1876

"Democracy and Literature," in *The Writings of John Burroughs: Literary Values and Other Papers*, John Burroughs, 1902

History of the Peloponnesian War, Thucydides, 5th century BC

Centennial Literary Reunion at the Residence of Horatio King, Horatio King, 1884

"Canadian Poetry and American Magazines, 1885-1905," James Doyle, 1979

"Regionalism and Local Color," Anne Rowe, in *Encyclopedia of Southern Culture*, eds. Charles Reagan Wilson and William Ferris, 1989

"American Literary Centres," in *Literature and Life*, William Dean Howells, 1902

"Later Poets," Norman Foerster, in Book III, Volume XVII, *The Cambridge History of English and American Literature*, eds. W. P. Trent, J. Erskine, S. P. Sherman, and C. Van Doren, 1907-1921

"The Later Novel: Howells," Carl Van Doren, in Book III, Volume XVII, *The Cambridge History of English and American Literature*, eds. W. P. Trent, J. Erskine, S. P. Sherman, and C. Van Doren, 1907-1921

On Prairie Winds, J.D. Eident and Timothy Taylor, 2015

Songs of Nature, ed. John Burroughs, 1901

ACKNOWLEDGMENTS

Appreciations will undoubtedly fall short, but they're worth the attempt.

Thank you to Tracey Williams and Melissa Agar, two high school teachers who recognized my capacity for writing and encouraged it long before I had a clue.

To Kurt Woock, who reads much of my work before anyone else and added insightful comments for this book. A better editor I have not met.

To Lynne Devlin at the Warren County Illinois Genealogical Society. Folks like her are known as genies for shorthand, but really it's because of their magic with research tools. Some of the great research tidbits here would not have come to light without her.

To several institutions where the staff helped me dig through the stacks: Rick Sayre, Hewes Library, Monmouth College; Kathy Nichols, Leslie F. Malpass Library, Western Illinois University; Zoe Norwood, Rockford Public Library; the State Library of Indiana; and the Library of Congress — its Chronicling America collection of digitized newspapers is divine.

To the Illinois Newspaper Project from the University of Illinois at Urbana-Champaign. The work of cataloging and digitizing the state's historic newspapers deserves more funding.

To Maura DeJaynes in the Warren County Clerk & Recorder office. She pulled all kinds of documents at my frequent requests.

To Brian Sterett, my uncle and the owner of a school.

And to the gracious hosts of the Maple City Writers Retreat. My parents tolerated me living at home and regaling them with tales of my daily gold-panning in decades of microfilm.

GOODIES

A proposal: I'll trade you a few intellectual candies if you'll go submit a review for this book online.

COLOPHON
This book uses Alegreya, a family of fonts designed by Juan Pablo del Peral.

TEN THINGS THAT HELPED FINISH THIS BOOK
MacBook laptop charger
Mozart's Symphony No. 29 in A Major
Warren County YMCA pool
plastic 4-H cup
Cubs baseball
brown chair in the living room
Tenderloin Tuesday
mortar mix
LEGOs
daily doses of *Pardon the Interruption*

ABOUT THE AUTHOR

Dustin Renwick fills his life with writing and competing in any sports events he can find. Usually, this choice involves running, but options like pickleball and the occasional limbo contest have made the list. His work has appeared in publications such as *The Washington Post* and *USA Triathlon*. Plus, *National Geographic* once selected his photo as an editor's pick. Check out more of his work at www.dustinrenwick.com.

Twitter: @drenwick110

Instagram: @swimbikerungram